CW01467977

Praise for *An Ecumenical .*

"Jakob Karl Rinderknecht has proven to be one of the most important and respected voices in ecumenical relations in the post-post-conciliar church. This critical edition and translation of Karl Rahner's *An Ecumenical Priesthood* not only validates this warranted reputation, but also represents an indispensable contribution to Anglophone discourse about the neuralgic themes of ministry, ordination, and sacramental theology that continue to plague our scandalous state of division within the Christian family. It belongs on every established and emerging ecumenist's bookshelf."

—Michael M. Canaris, associate professor of ecclesiology
and systematic theology, Loyola University Chicago;
executive board member, Karl Rahner Society

"Rahner's essay on ministry is a valuable and underappreciated contribution to ecumenical theology. Moreover, it's a gift to our own day as so many of us struggle to navigate disagreements more generally. How can we remain true to ourselves and our own traditions without just dismissing others? Rahner offers a window into his strategy for building bridges: digging for analogues, framing new questions, and making sure that the bridge in fact touches the two lands it seeks to connect. Jakob Rinderknecht has performed a great service by translating this work into English and offering such a helpful introduction."

—Brandon R. Peterson, associate professor, University of Utah, and author
of *Being Salvation: Atonement and Soteriology in the Theology of Karl Rahner*

"The publication in English of an untranslated work by Karl Rahner is a notable event. *An Ecumenical Priesthood* is especially welcome since its theme remains a 'live' issue for the church. As is true for his theology in general, Rahner addresses ordination and ministry in ways that are stimulating and challenging. Jakob Rinderknecht has given us a fine translation and an engaging introduction, bringing into relief Rahner's enduring importance."

—Richard Lennan, professor of systematic theology,
Boston College School of Theology and Ministry

"Jakob Karl Rinderknecht has done a great service by making this intriguing 1973 work by Karl Rahner available in English. It offers a fascinating peek into Rahner's thought processes as he lets his imagination experiment with possibilities for an ecumenical priesthood that go beyond church structures as they are and allow the Spirit to blow where she will. Grounded in the Catholic tradition and his understanding of the universal offer of grace, Rahner depicts an understanding of sacrament that can explicitly recognize the presence and activity of grace in Protestant ordinations. Although not a widely studied trajectory in Rahner's thought, ecumenism is both an explicit and implicit theme that culminates in the discussion of mutual recognition of ministries in the 1983 *Unity of the Churches: An Actual Possibility*.

"Rinderknecht's excellent critical introduction invites the reader to continue exploring the implications of this work for today's other pressing ecumenical issues that have intensified since the 1970s, such as ordination of women. The introduction also offers a lucid guide through the sometimes-meandering progress of Rahner's thought experiment.

"This is but a brief glimpse into a work that remains surprisingly timely for the ecumenical and ecclesial issues that continue to occupy us. Both the Rahner work and the Rinderknecht introduction merit the attention of all those engaged in these issues."

—Mary E. Hines, professor emerita of theology, Emmanuel College; author of *The Transformation of Dogma: An Introduction to Karl Rahner on Doctrine*; coeditor of *The Cambridge Companion to Karl Rahner*; former president of the Catholic Theological Society of America; and former member of the Anglican Roman Catholic Consultation in the United States

"In this exploratory work, Rahner reflects on the church's own life and sacramental practice, carefully distinguishing between the *ius divinum* and the *ius humanum* in order to allow the Catholic Church to recognize sacramental and saving grace outside its own canonical norms. Rahner's work on this question of ecumenical importance is a timely resource for thinking more expansively, creatively, and flexibly about the norms governing ordained sacramental ministry *within* the Catholic Church today. Rinderknecht's introduction to his translation is an indispensable map guiding the reader through Rahner's 'journey into the blue' on this *quaestio disputata*."

—Elyse Raby, assistant professor of religious studies, Santa Clara University

"Adding this newly translated work to Rahner's English corpus will hopefully reignite an ecumenical conversation that feels stalled for Catholics. Rahner gives Catholics an analogical path forward to recognize the reality of the ministry done by those ordained in other Christian denominations. The reason Rahner's works stand the test of time is that he is able to creatively reimagine solutions to issues such as the validity of ordination to the priesthood, while grounding his response in the tradition of the church."

—Heidi Russell, associate professor, Institute of Pastoral Studies at Loyola University Chicago, and author of *The Heart of Rahner*, *Quantum Theology*, and *Trinity and Catholicity*

"This work shines a light on the inadequacy of approaching the vexing question of the recognition of ministries through the classical categories of sacramental theology and canonical norms, and points to the need for new thinking that honors the graced reality present in the ecclesial life and ministries of Protestant communities. Rinderknecht's introduction helpfully contextualizes Rahner's reflections in the early stages of interchurch dialogue and argues convincingly for the need to better appreciate the extent to which his work is informed by ecumenical concern. The availability of this monograph in English translation is a welcome addition to contemporary discussion, coming at the precise moment when the issue of mutual recognition is emerging with even greater urgency, given advances in agreement on once church-dividing doctrines and the pressing need for shared witness in a deeply divided world."

—Catherine E. Clifford, Faculty of Theology, Saint Paul University

"With his insightful critical introduction and his crisp, accessible translation of an important work of Karl Rahner that has received too little attention in scholarly circles, Jakob Karl Rinderknecht has rendered a great service to the Christian community. Theologians, pastors, and those engaged in ecumenical dialogues will find in these pages an esteemed voice echoing across the decades to answer one of the most critical questions facing Christians today: what ministry ought to and can look like in the church of the twenty-first century."

—Peter Folan, SJ, assistant professor, Georgetown University, and author of *Martin Luther and the Council of Trent: The Battle over Scripture and the Doctrine of Justification*

An Ecumenical Priesthood

An Ecumenical
Priesthood

*The Spirit of God and the
Structure of the Church*

Karl Rahner

Translated with a Critical Introduction by
Jakob Karl Rinderknecht

Fortress Press
Minneapolis

AN ECUMENICAL PRIESTHOOD
The Spirit of God and the Structure of the Church

Copyright © 2022 in English translation by Fortress Press, an imprint of 1517 Media. All rights reserved. Except for brief quotations in critical articles or reviews, no part of this book may be reproduced in any manner without prior written permission from the publisher. Email copyright@1517.media or write Permissions, Fortress Press, PO Box 1209, Minneapolis, MN 55440-1209.

Karl Rahner, *Vorfragen zu einem ökumenischen Amtsverständnis* © 1974 Verlag Herder GmbH. Freiburg im Breisgau

Translated from the German by Jakob Karl Rinderknecht

Scripture quotations are from New Revised Standard Version Bible, copyright © 1989 National Council of the Churches of Christ in the United States of America. Used by permission. All rights reserved worldwide.

Cover design: Kristin Miller
Cover image: Consecration of the Bishop of Noyon with Scene of Pentecost Above, Pieter Claesz Soutman after Peter Paul Rubens, 1640-1657.

Print ISBN: 978-1-5064-8429-7
eBook ISBN: 978-1-5064-8430-3

Contents

A Note on Translation

This work is truly a glimpse into Karl Rahner's thought process—wide-ranging, grounded in the church's day-to-day experience, and convinced that the Spirit of God is working in the world. Throughout the piece, he is guided by his conviction that that Spirit is blowing among his Protestant colleagues and striving to give an account of that conviction that is both intelligible to other Catholics and honest about what he sees. At times, this leads him to almost hem and haw as he tries to keep the various pieces balanced. In translating it, I have tried to keep some of this sense of improvisation while also, by necessity, stipulating the connections more clearly due to the structure of English prose.

The German word *Amt* plays a major role throughout the piece. It means "office" but has a social sense of stability, bureaucracy, and power. Officeholders in the German churches are also government officials, as there is not the strict separation between church and state that Americans have come to expect. Because the more common descriptor of church offices in English (especially for describing Protestant officeholders) is "ministries," I have generally translated it in this way. One thing that gets lost is some of Rahner's wordplay, where he is holding together *Amt* (office) with *amtlich* (official) in considering the church's decisions in history as binding itself and its future. The reader can especially find this in the paragraphs toward the end of chapter 4.

Similarly, while he is playing with natural law ideas throughout the work, he is more directly talking about the church's law as arising from its unfolding experience of its own divinely given essence. When he talks about "essential law" or the church's constitution, he is there holding together all of these things, not merely referring to canon law or some subset thereof. Similarly, when he is discussing the pope's engagement with the church and other Christians, he is asking the reader to hold together the Catholic Church's self-conception (*Selbstverständnis*) and to recognize how natural and self-evident (*selbstverständlich*) this is in contrast with the effort it takes to think about the uncodified work of the Spirit outside of the visible bounds of the Catholic Church.

Rahner is very clear in this piece that it is not a polished, completed work ready for display. Instead, he is inviting the reader into the theologian's workshop to see the beginnings of a project take shape. The text itself reflects this. It is peppered with asides and parenthetical remarks—notes of what is only a possibility and what is more certain. One of the things that this has meant in translating the work is that I have often had to break down long, rambling sentences into paragraphs, sort out which referents refer to what, and generally impose order on Rahner's untidy workbench. I have sought to be faithful to Rahner's intention but encourage scholars to push aside the sawdust and consider Rahner's progress into the wild blue yonder themselves.

Jakob Karl Rinderknecht
San Antonio, Texas,
August 2022

Critical Introduction

Jakob Karl Rinderknecht

Publishing a new translation of one of Rahner's works nearly forty years after his death may seem like a strange task. When I've discussed this project with colleagues, the most common reaction has been surprise that there *are* still untranslated works by perhaps the most influential Roman Catholic theologian of the twentieth century. But *Vorfragen zu einem ökumenischen Amtsverständnis* is an outlier in Rahner's corpus. It is neither a full-length book like Rahner's *Foundations of Christian Faith*,[1] nor is it one of the essays for which he is so widely known and which are mostly collected in the volumes of *Theological Investigations*. Moreover, it is a work of speculative ecumenical theology, a genre in which Rahner was regularly engaged but which has remained understudied by succeeding scholars of his work.[2] Like most of Rahner's corpus, this book responded to a particular moment in the German academic conversation and is explicitly what Rahner calls "ein Fahrt ins Blaue," a thought experiment or a Sunday drive.

This book—to which I will refer here by the beginning of its German title, *Vorfragen*—initially appeared in 1973 in the Quaestiones Disputatae series published by Herder. That series, founded by

---

1. Karl Rahner, *Foundations of Christian Faith* (Freiburg: Herder, 1982).
2. Of the more than four thousand academic articles listing "Karl Rahner" as a keyword in the ATLA database, only twenty-five also list "ecumenism," and several of these are Rahner's own works.

Rahner and Heinrich Schleier in 1958, now has more than three hundred volumes. It provides "an academic forum for reflecting on questions in light of the breadth of theological disciplines and on the depth of theological challenges that are of the moment."[3]

Context is important for interpreting any book, but for this work, it is particularly critical. We must first understand why Rahner is concerned with *this* question (i.e., responding to the specific questions of his place and time, understood as "ein Fahrt ins Blaue"). But this seemingly minor byway has import beyond Germany in 1973—even beyond ecumenical theology in general. These questions are critical for understanding Rahner's thought overall. Understanding how he is accounting for the work of the Spirit among his Protestant brothers and sisters gives us a sense of how he sees the church relating to God and history to the eschaton. It also moves him to consider how the church's teaching accounts for experiences that do not fit its presuppositions. In fact, these questions occupied Rahner's final decade of life. His reflections in the *Vorfragen* ground a research trajectory that culminates in one of his last works, *Unity of the Churches: An Actual Possibility*, which he coauthored with Heinrich Fries in 1983.[4]

In the *Vorfragen*, Rahner considers how an authentically Roman Catholic theology, accepting magisterial teaching and its traditional judgments about the invalidity of Protestant ordinations, could account for its own experience of the work of the Spirit and the presence of grace among these same Protestant communities. In doing so, he proposes a means for recognizing the ordinations of

3. "Ein wissenschaftliches Forum, um in der Breite der theologischen Disziplinen und der Tiefe theologischer Herausforderungen Themen zu reflektieren, die an der Zeit sind." "Quaestiones Disputatae (107 Artikel)," Herder, accessed January 21, 2022, https://www.herder.de/theologie-pastoral-shop/reihen/quaestiones-disputatae/c-37/c-242/.
4. Heinrich Fries and Karl Rahner, *Unity of the Churches: An Actual Possibility*, trans. Ruth C. L. Gritsch and Eric W. Gritsch (Philadelphia: Fortress, 1983).

such communities as being authentic mediators of grace in the present without rejecting the historical judgment of invalidity. This is an interesting and important proposal, and one that deserves full consideration. It has only become more important since Rahner's death. In the last few decades, the primary theological issues separating Catholics and Protestants, especially the question of how sinners are justified before God, have been resolved. The ecclesiological issues however remain as *the* neuralgic questions for contemporary ecumenism. They are only made more difficult by the differences that have intensified between the communions in the last few decades regarding whether women can be priests and bishops. While Rahner does not provide an answer to this question about women in ministry, his work does provide a means of entering into the question in a way that both listens to the Catholic magisterial tradition and does not deny the reality of Protestant experience.

In order to guide the reader through this small but dense book, this introduction and commentary will first describe the immediate historical location in which the *Vorfragen* appeared. After doing so, it will then provide a brief overview to Rahner's argument and how it developed during the last decade of his life. Finally, it will consider how well the results of Rahner's thought experiment have weathered the nearly fifty years since it first appeared, a period in which the ecumenical landscape and the intra-Catholic responses to that landscape have changed significantly.

One final thing should be said about the *kind* of question that Rahner is asking. While it would be possible to ask about the same phenomena (Protestant pastors and bishops) in terms of their communal recognition, traditions of leadership, and an ethnographic description, this is not Rahner's question. Instead, he is facing *a properly theological question within a Roman Catholic milieu.* He recognizes how strange this whole question must seem for the Protestant reader. But he thinks that an authentic ecumenism requires "that each [side] attempts to understand the reality and self-understanding of the other church beginning from [its] own point of view."[5] The Protestant Christian not only will but *should* assume that their own Eucharist and ordination are "a self-evidently valid and legitimate fulfillment of Jesus's charge." But the Catholic ecumenist has a need and a duty to account for the work of God among their Protestant siblings, if only to give an account that allows other Catholics to authentically engage in the work of pursuing church unity. If progress is to be made, Catholic questions about Protestant communities must be answered in a way that *Catholics* recognize as belonging to their community's theology. And this means that Catholics cannot avoid the question of validity in this conversation. But any answers found will remain primarily of interest to Catholics as they account for their own ecumenical behavior.

If anything, since the 1970s, the question of a valid ministry has only become more important for ecumenical work. While the new distinction that arose out of the Second Vatican Council's *Unitatis redintegratio*, between "church" and "ecclesial community," was an attempt to make room between the all-and-nothing categories that had ruled Catholic discourse before the Second Vatican Council, it has itself become an ecumenical stumbling block. The Congregation for the Doctrine of the Faith has consistently, since the 1990s, interpreted the Second Vatican Council's distinction as being demarcated by the presence or absence of a Eucharist and a ministry that the Roman Catholic Church can recognize as valid.[6]

---

5. Karl Rahner, *Vorfragen zu einem ökumenischen Amtsverständnis*, in *Sämtliche Werke* (hereafter cited as SW), vol. 27, *Einheit in Vielfalt*, ed. Karl Lehmann and Albert Raffelt (Freiburg: Herder, 2002), 271.

6. The terms arise in chapter 3 of *Unitatis redintegratio*, November 21, 1964, https://www.vatican.va/archive/hist_councils/ii_vatican_council/documents/vat-ii_decree_19641121_unitatis-redintegratio_en.html. While the document refers to "Eastern Churches" and "Separated Churches and Ecclesial Communities in the West," in the years following the council, these two terms have been defined by the Congregation for the Doctrine of the Faith in a more restrictive way that

Among the problems with this account is that because a valid priesthood is understood by the Catholic Church to be necessary for a valid Eucharist, in practice, the question becomes one of valid ordination only. More importantly, although the Catholic Church recognizes the presence of grace in Protestant communities and in their liturgical actions,[7] and while an "ecclesial community" is not merely a "not-church," the category often collapses into a restatement of the preconciliar understanding of Protestants that it initially sought to overcome. Catholics have too often merely repeated the famous judgment about Anglican ordinations from Pope Leo XIII: that they are "absolutely null and utterly void."[8] This is clearly not the intent of *Unitatis redintegratio*, but too often Catholic figures insist that they cannot call Protestant communities "churches" without also noting that the Roman Catholic Church recognizes their communities as, properly speaking, "ecclesial."

This reproduces a problem with the category of (in)validity generally. *Validity* is primarily a legal term, not an ontological one. But it is commonly interpreted as a judgment of something's reality. As the Canon Law Centre defines the term, it "refers to the situation in law of an action performed in accordance with the law and recognized as producing the effects stipulated by law."[9] Invalidity is therefore not a judgment about the nonpresence of grace. It is a legal judgment that a particular act has not met the criteria that the

---

precludes understanding any of the communities arising from the Reformation as "churches." This definition, requiring a valid Eucharist and a valid priesthood according to Roman understanding, is most clearly spelled out in Congregation for the Doctrine of the Faith, "Communionis notio," May 28, 1992, §§17–18, https://www.vatican.va/roman_curia/congregations/cfaith/documents/rc_con_cfaith_doc_28051992_communionis-notio_en.html.

7. *Unitatis redintegratio* §3.

8. Pope Leo XIII, *Apostolicae curae*, Apostolic Letter, September 13, 1896, Acta Sanctae Sedis 29 (1896/97), 198–202, final para. (translation mine).

9. Canon Law Centre, *Glossary of Canonical Terms*, s.v. "valid," 2020, http://www.canonlawcentre.com/glossary-of-canonical-terms/.

church has set for recognizing that act. But it is an all-or-nothing, binary set of categories—and typical usage equates an invalid sacrament with an act devoid of grace (reflected in the judgment of Pope Leo XIII cited above: "absolutely null and utterly void"). In questions of law, this is necessary. I either am or am not married. I either own or do not own this house. But it is often the case that the world is more complex than the legal descriptions of it. And when we ask, "Is God acting here?" we particularly have to be observant regarding places where what we find to actually exist may not exactly comport to our initial expectations.

Because of these difficulties and how they have colored the Lutheran-Catholic conversation, Cardinal Ratzinger wrote to the Bavarian Lutheran bishop Johannes Hanselmann to argue that validity is an inadequate category for describing the Catholic understanding of the Lutheran Eucharist and the Lutheran community. While Catholic canonical requirements would lead to a judgment of invalidity if this is the question that is asked, Ratzinger reckons "as one of the important results of ecumenical conversations particularly the realization that the question of the Eucharist cannot be restricted to the problem of 'validity.' Even a theology along the lines of the concept of succession, as is in force in the Catholic and in the Orthodox Church, should in no way deny the saving presence of the Lord in the Evangelical Lord's supper."[10]

Similarly, by using the language of "ecclesial communities," *Unitatis redintegratio* clearly intends to describe Protestant communities as participating in the mystery of the one, holy, catholic and apostolic church, even if this is not a perfect participation. However, the category of validity is deeply entrenched in Catholic ways of thinking and is not easily overcome or set aside. Catholics have too many centuries of denying any reality to Protestant Eucharists

---

10. Joseph Ratzinger, "Letter to Bishop Johannes Hanselmann (March 9, 1993)," in *Pilgrim Fellowship of Faith: The Church as Communion* (San Francisco: Ignatius, 2005): 247–52.

or Protestant communities to easily adopt *Unitatis redintegratio*'s nuanced language without backsliding. Conversely, Protestants are generally able to recognize the Roman Church as a church while still believing that it is in need of ongoing reform. Rome's inability to fully reciprocate that recognition makes discussion of any ecclesiological topics difficult, especially since the recognition it does provide is regularly downplayed or misunderstood by Protestants and Catholics alike.

Moreover, because the question of valid ordination is central to the Catholic self-understanding, the question has become only more difficult to solve since Rahner wrote. Many Protestant churches have begun ordaining women as pastors and bishops since the 1970s. They generally see this practice as being a necessary implication of the gospel freedom of the church's new life in which "there is no longer Jew or Greek, there is no longer slave or free, there is no longer male and female" (Gal 3:28). The Roman Catholic Church, meanwhile, has repeatedly expressed the belief that the church is unable to ordain women.[11] While other questions of who the church *should* ordain (celibate or married, gay or straight, etc.) certainly complicate discussions of ordination, they finally fall into the realm of practice and pastoral judgment. But the Catholic insistence that the church is always and forever *unable* to validly ordain women makes this a unique barrier to the contemporary discussion.

In the *Vorfragen*, Rahner seeks to take this Catholic theological landscape seriously and respond to it in an unmistakably Catholic way. His thought experiment does not fully solve these problems.

---

11. While the position has been repeatedly stated by successive popes, the chief documents are Congregation for the Doctrine of the Faith, "Inter insignores," Declaration, October 15, 1976, https://www.vatican.va/roman_curia/congregations/cfaith/documents/rc_con_cfaith_doc_19761015_inter-insigniores_en.html; and Pope John Paul II, *Ordinatio sacerdotalis*, Apostolic Letter, May 22, 1994, https://www.vatican.va/content/john-paul-ii/en/apost_letters/1994/documents/hf_jp-ii_apl_19940522_ordinatio-sacerdotalis.html.

But it asks the questions involved in a new way, considering his contemporary situation of the divided church in light of God's final victory over every sin and every division, and asks where the movement of the Spirit might be discerned. If grace is God's self-communication, then places where God communicates Godself are "means of grace" and can be recognized as sacramental acts. And this perspective must change how we approach the question of sacramental validity.

Instead of attempting to do away with the question of sacramental validity, Rahner asks Catholics what resources within their tradition are available to make sense of complex cases like understanding contemporary Protestant communions. He asks Catholics if they are speaking completely truthfully about their Protestant siblings and whether there might be better questions to ask. Rahner wants Catholics to ask these new questions without losing track of their own concerns.

His considerations are not directly aimed at Protestant audiences. Nevertheless, entering into Rahner's experiment in charity might also prompt Protestants to understand the situation in a new way, or at least help them engage with their Catholic interlocutors in a new way. When ecumenical breakthroughs have occurred, they have often been the fruit of precisely such new questions. It is possible that Rahner's exploration of the byroads and the countryside could help us discover another way forward.

Historical Location of the *Vorfragen*

In order to see that potential road, we need to begin by understanding where Rahner stood when he was trying to point it out. The early 1970s saw a number of bilateral ecumenical dialogues on questions related to the ordained ministry, including the Anglican–Roman Catholic International Commission (ARCIC), the US Lutheran-Catholic Dialogue, the International Lutheran–Roman Catholic Dialogue, the Groupe des Dombes, and the Faith and

Order Commission.[12] However, the most important piece of context for the *Vorfragen* is the publication in 1973 of a memorandum on the question of whether the major Christian communions in Germany could mutually recognize one another's ministries. It was published by five German ecumenical institutes and lists twenty-four contributors.[13] It received quite a few responses from both theologians and church leadership.

The memorandum is not a bilateral document in the usual sense—it was not the product of a commission appointed by the churches. Instead, it was the academic proposal of a group of ecumenically minded theologians. It did not see its purpose as examining the classical differences in teaching nor in expounding a complete teaching on ordination.[14] For example, the document lacks a consideration of the various levels of ministry and their necessity and does not attempt to solve the historical differences in understanding the relationship of the ordained ministry to the common priesthood of the baptized. Instead, it is an attempt to

---

12. English versions of all of these texts are available in *Modern Ecumenical Documents on the Ministry* (London: SPCK, 1975). For the original French of the Groupe des Dombes, see Groupe des Dombes, *Pour une réconciliation des ministères* (Taizé: Les Presses de Taizé, 1973).

13. *Reform und Anerkennung kirchlicher Ämter: Ein Memorandum der Arbetisgemeinschaft ökumenischer Universitätsinstitute* (Munich: Kaiser, 1973). The institutes involved were Bochum, Heidelberg, Munich, Münster, and Tübingen. The contributing theologians are listed below, with the directors of the involved institutes in italics:

Johannes Brosseder, Matthias Fomm, *Heinrich Fries*, Gotthard Fuchs, Elisabeth Gast, Hans-Jürgen Goertz, Hermann Häring, Eberhard Hassler, Konrad Klesse, Friedhelm Krüger, *Hans Küng, Peter Lengsfeld*, Reinhard Leuze, Knut Mackensen, Peter Neuner, Josef Note, *Wolfhart Pannenberg*, Michael Raske, *Edmund Schlink*, Günter Schnurr, Joachim Schwarz, Yorick Spiegel, Michael Stanislaus, and *Hans-Heinrich Wolf*.

14. Wolfhart Pannenberg, "Ökumenische Einleitung über die gegenseitige Annerkennung der kirchlichen Ämter: Zu den Intentionen des Memorandums der ökumenischen Universitätsinstitute," *Catholica* 28, no. 2 (1974): 142.

"express the positive consensus of the involved institutes as theses for understanding ecclesial office."[15]

The document stirred up quite a bit of response, both positive and negative, especially from church officials. The response of the German bishops' doctrinal commission was particularly negative. While the bishops pointed to the partial consensus on church ministries that was emerging from the bilateral and multilateral dialogues, they argued that the memorandum took an inappropriate approach to both history and exegesis that ignored both the development of the faith and the consensus of the faith in East and West in the early postapostolic era. In particular, they condemn the memorandum for specifically avoiding any engagement with the Catholic approach to ministry.[16]

In this context, Rahner's project becomes clearer. There was a developing partial consensus on the theology of ministry. A number of practical theological problems remained, which demonstrated the particular asymmetry that is not uncommon in ecumenical questions: the question that was so important to one party (Catholics' requirement that "churches" must have valid ministries) did not have a direct analog on the other side. It was not the simple kind of question to which both sides had parallel commitments and arguments developed and honed over time. Instead, because of their different commitments, this question was more central for one communion than it was for the other.

15. "Das Memorandum versucht, den positiven Konsensus der beteiligten Institute in gemeinsamen Thesen zum Verständnis des kirchlichen Amtes auszusprechen." Pannenberg, 142.
16. Glaubenskommission der Bischöfe, "Stellungnahme," *Herder Korrespondenz* 27 (1973): 159.

Overview of the Argument

Rahner repeatedly emphasizes that the work is truly a *quaestio disputata*, just as the series title promises. In the introductory section, he frames the work as a view into the theologian's workshop. He is not presenting a finished work but the initial attempt. Rather than doing what the theologian usually does and guiding his reader down a well-scouted path, Rahner invites us to join him on a Sunday drive into the wilds of a contemporary question: exploring the territory, asking new questions, seeing where the lesser-traveled paths might lead.

In doing so, he is framing his work against both the kind of scholastic thinker who knows the answer before a new question is posed and those who see in his work a dismissal of historical theology. In the latter camp, Rahner names at least Hans Küng, with whom he had had a difficult series of interactions over the previous several years.[17] Rahner's scathing public response in 1970 to Küng's *Infallible? An Inquiry* led to the rebuttal from Küng that Rahner cites here and angrily dismisses.[18] Rahner then insists that history *of itself* tells us nothing unless we ask it questions. And so, our questions are necessary—not only for framing speculative theology but for rightly practicing historical theology itself.

The dispute with Küng is perhaps more illuminating of the tightrope that Rahner is attempting to cross here than would be otherwise immediately apparent. Both authors are investigating ideas central to the contemporary Roman Catholic account of the church in light of difficulties posed by history, theological concerns,

---

17. See chapter 1.
18. K. Rahner, "Kritik an Hans Küng: Zur Frage der Unfehlbarkeit theologischer Sätze," *Stimmen der Zeit* 186, no. 12 (December 1970): 361–77; and H. Küng, "Im Interesse der Sache: Antwort an Karl Rahner," *Stimmen der Zeit* 187, no. 1 (January 1971): 43–64. For a good overview of the argument there, see J. J. Hughes, "Infallible? An Inquiry Considered," *Theological Studies* 32, no. 2 (1971): 183–207.

and the German ecumenical situation. Both are trying to make the contemporary world sensible in light of that history. Their commitments, however, are quite different.

One way to misread their dispute would be to cast it as being about whether *Humanae vitae* is right or wrong.[19] This is not the case, however. Where Küng sees *Humanae vitae* as claiming infallibility and having been proven wrong—and therefore as an example of the problems of infallibility—Rahner instead sees a document that, while not changing the church's recent teaching on the subject, is not *itself* an infallible *ex cathedra* teaching, nor does it point to a teaching that has fulfilled the conditions of the infallibility of the ordinary universal magisterium laid down in *Lumen gentium* §25. Rahner does not answer whether *Humanae vitae* is right or wrong (though he believes that Küng has not bothered to prove his case for its falsity). He argues instead that *Humanae vitae* does not intend to teach something definitively. Instead, it is a conventional document that neither intends to nor actually does teach infallibly. It therefore cannot stand as an example of the case for which Küng has called it to witness.[20]

Rahner is convinced that there exists an account of development that can be harmonized with the idea that some aspects of the church are *de iure divino* (according to divine law), even though they developed in history. This makes itself felt in the dispute with Küng, including Rahner's judgment that a conversation with *Infallible? An Inquiry* could no longer be called "an intra-Catholic conversation."[21]

What does this have to do with the present work, which concerns itself with neither contraception nor papal infallibility? In the

---

19. Rahner, "Kritik an Küng," 365: "Die Kontroverse über Küngs These kann man von der Sache her nicht mehr als eine inner-katholische theologische Kontroverse betrachten."

20. Rahner, 368.

21. Küng is aware of and dismisses this aspect of Rahner's thought. See especially his *Theology for the Third Millennium: An Ecumenical View*, trans. Peter Heinegg (New York: Doubleday, 1988), 186–88.

Vorfragen, Rahner must walk a careful way between on the one hand rejecting magisterial teachings that understand themselves to be definitive judgments about the ordinations of Protestant Christians and on the other becoming blind to the working of the Holy Spirit among Protestants (and therefore rejecting the authoritative teaching of the Second Vatican Council).[22]

Rahner's position on the possibility of authentic developments arising in history and becoming necessary to the church (and thus truly *de iure divino*) is well documented in a number of essays.[23] But the *Vorfragen* asks a slightly different question: What happens in the wake of a schism that has led Roman authorities to definitively judge that communion was broken in such a way that its separated brethren's congregations have become "not-churches"? In this situation, is God powerless to act to heal these communities outside of the "regular" action of canonical procedure? Should God do so, how would we know and judge that this has taken place? And can contemporary ecclesial authority change its understanding of what happened in light of God's action in the world? Or do we have to say that the earlier judgments were wrong in order to move forward?

Taking this work as an attempt at a difficult question, a *quaestio disputata,* Rahner is exploring how a properly Roman Catholic argument can be made about God's work in Protestant ministries. At several points, he recognizes that this argument may seem strange

---

22. Of course, on the one side most famously stands the declaration on Anglican order and also the clear canonical argument that presbyteral ordination is invalid. On the other stands *Unitatis redintegratio* §3 with its judgment that the liturgical rites of the separated brethren are "capable of giving access to that communion in which is salvation."

23. See, especially, K. Rahner, "Reflection on the Concept of *ius divinum* in Catholic Thought," in *Theological Investigations* (hereafter cited as *TI*), vol. 5 (Baltimore: Darton, Longman & Todd, 1966), 219–43, originally published as Rahner, "Über den Begriff des *jus divinum* im katholischen Verständnis," in *Schriften zur Theologie,* vol. 5 (Einsiedeln: Benzinger Verlag, 1962), 249–77.

or even offensive to the Protestants involved, who need no proof of the working of the Spirit in their midst and through their pastors. But given the canonical and ecclesiastical structure of the Catholic Church, answering this question is necessary for ecumenical healing if Catholics are to recognize Protestants' communities as truly Christian churches. An intra-Catholic account is required as to how *both* the historical judgment of the invalidity of Protestant ordinations *and* a contemporary recognition of the effectiveness of those orders can possibly be true.

There is a tantalizing parallel here to the claims of the *Joint Declaration on the Doctrine of Justification* (*JDDJ*).[24] That document, in recognizing the noncontradiction between Lutheran and Catholic descriptions of the justification of the sinner and their sanctification, explicitly notes that it is not undoing the doctrinal condemnations made in the sixteenth century. Instead, it lets them stand as "salutary warnings" against truly false teaching.[25] Instead, the churches state that "the teaching of the Lutheran churches presented in this Declaration does not fall under the condemnations from the Council of Trent. The condemnations in the Lutheran Confessions do not apply to the teaching of the Roman Catholic Church presented in this Declaration."[26] The judgments of the churches in the sixteenth century are recognized as *both* true *and* not applicable to the present consensus. The parties recognize both a real agreement with the other and their own continuity with the binding judgments of their predecessors.

This is a much easier question to balance regarding the teaching on justification, however, than it is on the recognition of ordination. Rahner cannot merely say, "the practice of ordination that was ruled invalid in the sixteenth century wasn't actually the Lutheran

---

24. Roman Catholic Church and the Lutheran World Federation, *The Joint Declaration on the Doctrine of Justification* (*JDDJ*) (Grand Rapids: Eerdmans, 2000).

25. *JDDJ* §42.

26. *JDDJ* §41.

or Anglican or other Protestant practice." The particular ordinations judged were specifically those ordinations. The intention of
the Roman authorities was to judge that precisely those communities had fallen into schism with Rome and were not practicing
a recognizable ordination to priesthood and episcopacy. And if
those ordinations were invalid, then according to canonical logic, any
ordinations dependent on them must also be judged invalid. And
so it seems that the necessary position becomes, as one of my
former classmates put it, "At some point you have to determine
whether Protestants were validly ordained. And it seems that the
church has." This, then, is the disputed and difficult terrain that
Rahner sets himself to explore.

Outline

The book is arranged in six chapters and ends with an appended
excursus on the question of intercommunion:

1. Asking the Question, Imagining an Answer
2. The Essence of the Church's Structure
    2.1. Initial Considerations
    2.2. Where the Juridical Account of the Church Fails
    2.3. The Nature of the Church Unfolding in History
3. Recognizing Reality
4. Sharing Salvation
    4.1. Good and Bad Faith in a Time of Schism
    4.2. Grace Outside of the Norm
5. Form, Validity, and History
6. Bearing Our Divisions on the Way to Unity
Appendix: An Excursus on Intercommunion
    Methodology
    Current Church Norms on Intercommunion
    Principles Embedded in These Norms
    Norms to Guide Current Practice

Rahner argues for a way of thinking about the church's nature that starts with examining its actual history and attending to examples of its decisions and behaviors in historical context. Rahner is committed to the Aristotelian position that we discover the possible from the real and not the real from the possible.[27] The rubber of this claim hits the road in section 2.2. His title for this section, when revised into a thesis, becomes "We Cannot Ascribe or Ground All of Church Law and the Church's Legal Acts in Merely the Historic Succession of the Episcopate and the Primacy of Peter."[28] In other words, we cannot merely think as lawyers who look backward to found the church's actions in the actions of the hierarchy. God does new things and grace comes to the church from outside. We must ground our account in God rather than solely in the ecclesial structures that depend on God.

This responds to an argument implied by the standard account of the validity of ordination. If we think of ecclesiality as arising from (or being predicated on) an unbroken chain of valid ordinations, then we set up at least the implication that this chain of valid ordinations must go back to the beginning of the church. Indeed, the implication is so strong that *Lumen gentium*'s description of the episcopacy as descending from the apostles "per successionem ab initio decurrentem" (*Lumen gentium* 20; by a succession running from the beginning) gets rendered in several of the major English translations as "by an *unbroken* succession from the beginning."[29]

27. Karl Rahner, "The Development of Dogma," in *TI*, 1:41, originally published as "Zur Frage der Dogmenentwicklung," *Wissenschaft und Weltbild* 7 (1954): 1–14, 94–106.

28. The German title is "Unrückführbarkeit allen Rechtes auf Primat und Episkopat."

29. So, for example, "and in virtue consequently of the unbroken succession, going back to the beginning." This is the translation in Flannery, and it is picked up in the *Catechism of the Catholic Church*, 2nd ed. (Vatican City: Libreria Editrice Vaticana, 1997), §1555. The Latin of the *Catechism* follows the wording of *Lumen gentium*.

Rahner attributes his recognition of this problem to a discussion for which he was present at Vatican II. The editors of the *Sämtliche Werke* edition of *Vorfragen*, Karl Cardinal Lehmann and Albert Raffelt, posit that perhaps this was the ecclesiological subcommission Va (*De collegio et ministeriis Episcoporum*).[30] In this context, he notes that when the council affirms that the College of Bishops operates legally only when it does so in concert with the pope (as in the *Nota explicativa praevia*), this is sensible. But we quickly come to a contradiction if we try to make too maximalist of an interpretation derive from this. So for example, Rahner asks, if this were always and everywhere the case, how could the College of Cardinals ever validly elect a pope, since they are by necessity operating without a pope whenever they do so?[31]

Similarly, Rahner asks how understanding this historical development changes our method of proceeding to consider non-Catholic Christian ministers. If particular developments happened within the Roman Church such that things that once were optional are now considered necessary, might it be possible that other Christians with differentiable histories might be determined to have developed such that other conditions were recognized as necessary within their communions?[32] Certainly something like this is operative in contemporary Catholic consideration of the Eastern Churches, for whom Catholics make no difficulty over sacramental validity, despite many differences in ecclesial and sacramental law and practice. Whether such differences might be recognized in the Protestant churches, where the historical separation is both more recent and more controverted, remains an open question. But if it is indeed a *quaestio disputata*, then Rahner's initial considerations cannot merely be dismissed.

---

30. See note h in section 2.2.
31. See argument section 2.2.
32. See argument section 2.3.

A final major question that Rahner proposes is this: How can we be certain that any particular chain of ordinations is without a break that would render the entire dependent chain invalid? In considering the difficulties, he concludes,

> How does, for example, a priest know that he is validly ordained? If he predicates this validity only on a unbroken chain of valid ordinations (validity being understood in the usual way) beginning with the bishop who ordained him and stretching back to the apostles, considering the conditions of validity according to the usual measures (including also internal intention, perhaps in the Middle Ages the very particular traditio instrumentorum, and the many other terms that apply or have applied), then this priest must say that (morally) he, at the very best, can presume a likelihood for the validity of his ordination. He must trust to the benevolent providence of God that there have not been too many invalid ordinations in this extensive ordination chain, since the conditions set for a valid ordination can be easily disrupted without anyone noticing.[33]

Validity by its very nature is much easier to disprove than it is to prove, especially in considering the question of the internal intention of a minister other than oneself. In response to this problem, the church gives the benefit of the doubt to the intention of the minister of a sacrament, presuming that the external requirements of matter and form are in place.

This is, for example, the contention of Leo XIII in his judgment about Anglican ministries, *Apostolicae curae*, at §33:

> Therefore, most closely joined to the defect of form is the defect of intention, which is understood to be of equal

---

33. See chapter 3.

necessity in determining that something is indeed a sacrament. Concerning the mind or intention, insofar as these are essentially interior, the church does not pass judgment, but to the extent it is manifested externally, a judgment is required. And so, a person who has correctly and seriously used the requisite matter and form to confect and confer a sacrament is presumed for that very reason to have intended to do what the church does. On this reasonable principle rests the doctrine which holds there to be a true sacrament or the like, which ministered by a heretical person or a non-baptized person so long as the Catholic rite is conferred. On the other hand, if the rite be changed, with the manifest intention of introducing another rite not approved by the Church and of rejecting what the Church does, and what, by the institution of Christ, belongs to the nature of the Sacrament, then it is clear that not only is the necessary intention lacking to the Sacrament, but that there is intention adverse to and destructive of the Sacrament.[34]

However, Rahner's difficulty is not fully answered by this, for the canonical response is necessarily about a single sacramental act.

---

34. "Cum hoc igitur intimo formae defectu coniunctus est defectus intentionis, quam aeque necessario postulat, ut sit, sacramentum. De mente vel intentione, utpote quae per se quiddam est interius, Ecclesia non iudicat: at quatenus extra proditur, iudicare de ea debet. Iamvero quum quis ad sacramentum conficiendum et conferendum materiam formamque debitam serio ac rite adhibuit, eo ipso censetur id nimirum facere intendisse quod facit Ecclesia. Quo sane principio innititur doctrina quae tenet esse vere sacramentum vel illud, quod ministerio hominis haeretici aut non baptizati, dummodo ritu catholico, conferatur. Contra, si ritus immutetur, eo manifesto consilio ut alius inducatur ab Ecclesia non receptus, utque id repellatur quod facit Ecclesia et quod ex institutione Christi ad naturam attinet sacramenti, tunc palam est, non solum necessariam sacramento intentionem deesse, sed intentionem immo haberi sacramento adversam et repugnantem." Leo XIII, *Apostolicae curae*, para. 11.

Whether the ordinations of all of the persons in the chain leading to one's own ordination in the present were ordained with proper matter and form remains unprovable. Both the multiplication of historical cases and their ever-growing distance from the present means that this must remain a matter of faith for the church.

Rahner's solution is to suggest that "the valid ordination of a priest or bishop is present if he is recognized as such by the church without dissent."[35] Whether this is a workable canonical definition or not, it is a good practical description of how the question is handled, particularly for intra-Catholic (and Catholic to Orthodox) considerations. No healthy person wastes too much time worrying that the faults of some unknown bishop in the early Middle Ages means that their entire ministry is invalid. Because one can recognize that those who ordained them a priest (or a bishop) did so in good faith and with the universal support of the church, the presumption must be that the ordination is valid, even if there is a not-zero and not-negligible chance of a failure of intent or minister or matter or form somewhere along the inaccessible historical chain. But even had that been the case, we can judge from the fruits of what we do know that within the church, this failure has been overcome. *Ecclesia supplet.*

And so Rahner asks whether it might be possible for Catholics to make a similar kind of judgment on behalf of Protestants. Certainly more proof would be required, because instead of worrying about the possibility of a break, we know that in these cases the church *has* judged the chain to have been broken. Any healing would have to fall outside of the normal mode of reasoning. It is at this point that Rahner begins his extended analogy to marriage law and to the possibility of a kind of radical sanation, a canonical judgment that an invalid sacrament has been healed "at the root."

---

35. See chapter 3.

An Unexpected Tool: *Radical Sanation*

The idea of *sanatio in radice* has roots that trace back to the High Middle Ages, although some authors trace its history (in truth, if not in name) back to the Council of Orleans (511) or to the Councils of Agde (506) or Epaon (517). This view was put forward first by Giovanni Perrone, SJ, in 1858. This position did not gain significant traction among canonists, although it is always mentioned in treatments of the topic.[36] Whether we can say that the canons of these councils are truly *sanatio in radice* is not important to understanding Rahner. However, it is interesting to notice that the problem to which *sanatio in radice* is a solution is as old as church law, even if the exact understanding of how such a solution is understood to be possible changes.

As cultural norms about marriage differ, so many of the early conciliar declarations that look like radical sanations were offered primarily for groups who had converted to Christianity but who had customs of allowing marriage within closer degrees of consanguinity.[37] The councils in question therefore ruled that these marriages (contracted before the council) would be considered valid, although any new marriages contracted in this way would remain invalid.

In the medieval period, the radical validation of marriages shifts in its focus. Instead of dealing with cultural difference and adaptation to Christianity, the central question becomes the retroactive legitimation of children, and this is where the most unique aspect of radical sanation emerges. Unlike what would come to be the more

---

36. So, for example, Thomas Charles Ryan, *Juridical Effects of the Sanatio in Radice: A Historical Synopsis and a Commentary* (Washington, DC: Catholic University of America Press, 1955), 8–10; and Peter Fabritz, *Sanatio in Radice: Historie eines Rechtsinstituts und seine Beziehung zum sakramentalen Eheverständnis der katholischen Kirche* (New York: Peter Lang, 2009), 61–92.

37. Ryan, *Juridical Effects*, 8–10.

typical means of repairing an invalidly contracted marriage (a new declaration of intent after the impediment has been removed), a "perfect" decree of *sanatio in radice* (under the code of 1917, in effect when Rahner wrote) contains three legislative acts:

1. a dispensation or cessation of the impediment that prevented a valid marriage,
2. a dispensation from the law requiring a renewal of consent, and
3. a retroaction "by a fiction of the law" regarding canonical effects to the past.[38]

It may be helpful to quickly consider each of these and what the analogous concerns are in Rahner's proposal regarding contemporary Protestant ministries.

Cessation of the Impediment
The decree of *sanatio in radice*, when "perfect" or containing all the aspects found in can. 1138 of the 1917 Code of Canon Law, provides a dispensation of the impediment that prevented the marriage from being valid in the first place. But not all impediments may be dispensed, only those that are breaches in ecclesiastical law (such as insufficient age, prior vows of chastity, or wider degrees of consanguinity). Impediments understood to arise out of divine law (such as previous marriage, close consanguinity, or impotence) cannot be dispensed and must have ceased before such a decree may come into effect.[39]

---

38. Code of Canon Law (hereafter cited as CIC) 1917, 1138. Unless otherwise indicated, translations will be taken from Edward N. Peters, ed., *The 1917 Pio-Benedictine Code of Canon Law: In English Translation with Extensive Scholarly Apparatus* (San Francisco: Ignatius, 2001).
39. Robert J. Harrington, *The Radical Sanation of Invalid Marriages, an Historical Synopsis and Commentary* (Washington, DC: Catholic University of America Press, 1938), 37, 99–104; and Ryan, *Juridical Effects*, 3–4. The question of whether the

Rahner does not doubt the church's judgment that the post-Reformation ordinations were invalid and so asks on what basis this is true. He begins with an assumption arising from *Unitatis redintegratio* §3, which both recognizes blame for the schism in the sixteenth century "on both sides" and asserts that *contemporary* Protestants cannot be held blameworthy for the schism: "One must, so it appears to me, first carefully ponder the fact that one ought to differentiate between the relationship of the Catholic Church to the other churches in the moment of the *origination* (according to the Catholic view) of heretical or schismatic churches, and the relationship that exists in a later age when these churches are no longer to be primarily understood in terms of their denial of the Catholic Church and/or its teachings."[40] Asserting this distinction quickly sets the stage to ask what made post-Reformation ordinations invalid from a Catholic perspective and to consider whether this condition is still active among Protestants or whether their ordinations are judged invalid merely because the chain of validity has been broken. In other words, Rahner asks whether the impediment that led to the original judgment of invalidity still exists or has been overcome.

In the sixteenth century, assuming that the primary issue is one of schism, Rahner diagnoses the root cause as mala fides toward the Roman Church.[41] Schism, perhaps uniquely, is a sin of broken relationship mediated only by the will. It exists because those involved believe it to exist and act as if it exists. Rahner points to the differences between how Catholic and Protestant leaders acted toward each other in the immediate wake of schism and how they

---

church may grant a radical sanation in cases of divine law *after* the cessation of the impediment is also unsurprisingly disputed. See John P. Beal, "The Convalidation of Marriage," in *New Commentary on the Code of Canon Law*, ed. Beal, James A. Coriden, and Thomas J. Green (Mahwah, NJ: Paulist, 2000), 1387–88.

40. See section 4.1.

41. At this point, Rahner is careful to once again note that he is thinking about Protestants *as a Roman Catholic*, making arguments for Catholics about how to understand the relationship of non-Catholic Christians to the Roman Church.

act in the twentieth century as proof that the mala fides that constituted the sixteen-century schism between Rome and Protestants
are no longer in effect. Therefore, there is no longer a total separation. This is visible in the ways that the Second Vatican Council,
and the Roman Catholic Church as a whole since then, speaks of
Protestants. They are "separated brethren," not "heretics and schismatics." As Rahner points out, "The churches are separated, but it
is recognized that they are not separated today by an act occurring
here and now."[42]

None of this is to say that there might not still be disagreements
that rise to the level of being church-dividing between Christians.
Rahner suggests that one of these issues might be the role of the
papacy, for example. But for the sake of the thought experiment,
Rahner lays these questions aside to ask whether, in a situation
where there was understood to be a division of an inherited schism
but not of church-dividing theology, the Catholic Church could
recognize the ministries of the Protestants without requiring the
(re)ordination of all of their ministers.

And so in this case (and in our thought experiment), the original
impediment, mala fides toward the Roman Church (the root cause
of schism), is understood as having been fully overcome. It is here
that the analogy to radical sanation becomes helpful to Rahner.
This canonical decree recognizes that there had truly been a real
impediment and that nevertheless, by the grace of God, the fruits
of the sacrament are present. As Rahner comments, "The *sanatio in
radice* merely recognizes explicitly that the lack of form which had
appeared to make the marriage impossible in this case had not done
so; the lawgiver does not change the thing itself, but defines his own
relationship to it."[43]

---

42. See section 4.1.
43. See chapter 3.

Dispensation from Renewed Consent and Retroaction of Effects
Rahner is considering the social and ecclesial effects of the declaration, not following a canonical construal of what is important in the
question. For him, the church's recognition of the marriage existing
without a new consent, which amounts to recognizing the fruits of
the marriage, is central. For the canonist, however, this is parsed out
in terms of a "dispensation from renewed consent" and "retroaction of effects," both of which describe the situation not from the
point of view of the couple (who may not have even known that
their marriage was deemed invalid or that the decree rectifying this
problem was granted) but from that of the expositor of the law.[44]

The utility of the proposal in the ecumenical realm is clear—it
would allow the Roman Church to rearticulate its relationship to the
pastors and bishops within Protestant communions without requiring that all of these persons be (re)ordained. Why is this important? Because while the idea of canonical validity of ordination is
more important in Roman Catholic thought about the church than
among most Protestants, there are a variety of related ideas present
within all of the groups arising from the sixteenth-century reforma-
tions. For all of them, saying, "We have overcome our theological
difficulties. All that remains is for you to be reordained," would be
akin to asking them to admit that the Spirit had not been active in
their own ministries and in those who brought them to the gospel.
It is also a potent symbol of the "return ecumenism" of the past

44. One of the things that seems clear to me in reading this history is that radical
sanation is, throughout its history, a pastoral act in response to particular cases in
which church authorities decide to act. The canonical argument about what is
possible and what is *actually happening* is always after the fact, controverted, and regularly ignored by those in authority when making their decisions. So, for example,
when the Holy Office declared in 1904 that the church lacks the power to grant
radical sanation in cases of divine law impediments, Pope Pius X weakened this in
canon law to a statement that it was not done (not impossible) and church practice
continued to grant them until they were once again formalized legally in 1966. See
Beal, "Convalidation of Marriage," 1387–88.

that sees unity with Rome as requiring individual return to not only communion with Rome but the forms and law of the Roman Rite.[45]

Retroaction

And so in this situation, what radical sanation offers is an analogous case, one in which the church's law recognizes that its recognition of a changed situation, potentially without the knowledge or consent of the parties involved, causes a change to how history is understood.[46] However, the canonical perspective on radical sanation described above does not directly answer the pastoral/existential reception or effects of such a decree. These are worth considering in more depth.

Because a radical sanation uniquely includes the retroaction of canonical effects into the past, canonists have argued at length about how exactly this is possible and what it means. In the case of marriage, of course, the primary effect that such a retroaction has is the legitimation of children born of the sanated marriage; this is the primary purpose for which the writ was invented. Within canonical discussions, particularly during the period Rahner is writing, much was hung on the phrase "by a fiction of the law" (*per fictionem iuris*) that is found in the 1917 code's description of radical sanation.[47] Because a radical sanation is a legal decree, what it achieves is canonical—that is, pertaining to law. What is retroacted

---

45. For a brief history, see Jeffrey Gros, Eamon McManus, and Ann Riggs, *Introduction to Ecumenism* (Mahwah, NJ: Paulist, 1998), 25–32.

46. "Consent" here should be understood as consent to the church's action, not consent to the marriage. Radical sanation relies on the understanding that the consent to the marriage has authentically been given. But in some cases, for example, a spouse might not consent to giving a new consent (because they do not believe that it is necessary or because they are unable, as may happen in cases of mental decline) and so a simple convalidation is not possible. In this case, a radical sanation is possible. See Beal, "Convalidation of Marriage," 1390.

47. The "fiction of the law" clause falls away in the 1983 code text, although it is still cited in some commentaries on the new code. See Beal, 1388.

are the legal effects—the past is not changed, but how that past is interpreted and received, is. Attending to how canonists talk about this question and how Rahner describes the same reality from a different viewpoint will help clarify what Rahner is and is not arguing in the *Vorfragen*.[48]

Canonists historically framed their argument around the effects of radical sanation by asking what happened "ex nunc" (from now), and what happened "ex tunc" (from then). The question often blends legal questions with arguments about cause and effect in the world. In a representative argument, Thomas Ryan disagrees with the position of Robert Harrigan about what this retroaction means:

> Harrigan confuses the effects of marriage as such with the canonical effects of matrimony. His position leads to conclusions that cannot possibly be sustained or accepted. Following his statement to its logical conclusion, one would necessarily have to hold that the sacramental grace conferred by the sacrament of matrimony is granted retroactively to the parties. Thus it would be effective at the inception of the invalid marriage. This conclusion obviously is theologically impossible. Since the convalidation is effective *ex nunc*, the sacrament is received *ex nunc*, and hence the sacramental grace also. Under no circumstances could sacramental grace be construed as being conferred apart from a sacrament being

---

48. In previous writings on this topic, I speculated about this retroaction being itself the fruit of the church's decision. I now believe that this is both unhelpful and unnecessary. Instead, a better reading of Rahner here sees the church changing its verdict on the contemporary fruits of the sacrament in light of new information. Clearly, the actor here is God, and if the gratuitous fruits of divine grace exist where there was an act deemed an invalid sacrament before, God's action is still not dependent on the church's recognition. The recognition follows from God's previous and fully gratuitous action apart from the usual order God desires for the church. See my "Order out of Order: Rahner's Tectonic Proposal for an Ecumenical Difficulty," *Horizons* 42, no. 2 (2015): 341–67.

conferred also. Harrigan's statement would also mean that the conjugal rights would be granted to the parties retroactively. The metaphysical impossibility of such an event has already been discussed.[49]

Notice particularly the portion in the middle arguing about why logic dictates that only canonical effects are retroacted by the decree of sanation (a plain-text reading of the code). Ryan then shifts gears and argues from necessity that "under no circumstances could sacramental grace be construed as being conferred apart from a sacrament being conferred also." This certainty misunderstands (by overreach) what a declaration of invalidity is and in effect limits God's actions *by necessity* to the recognized sacraments within the church. This position is impossible to square with the recognitions in *Lumen gentium, Nostra aetate, Unitatis redintegratio*, and *Gaudium et spes* of God's action for the salvation of the world outside the visible bounds of the Roman Catholic Church.

Rahner, reasoning about the same set of circumstances, begins with different questions and therefore gets different answers. For Rahner, the idea that grace (and even grace-filled participation in the finalities to which sacraments give access) is present outside of the sacraments is not an absurdity but a clear truth. Ryan is simply wrong about the impossibility of sacramental grace being found apart from the sacraments. Rahner's contrary assumption reflects the positions of the Second Vatican Council as it reasoned about non-Catholic Christians and about non-Christian persons. The heart of this insight lives in *Unitatis redintegratio* §3, which carefully considers how the Roman Catholic Church's claim that the one Church of Christ subsists in it in a unique way (*Lumen gentium* §8) can coexist with an honest recognition of the presence of God in the communities of the separated brethren, such that their (invalid) liturgical actions can "engender a life of grace" and

---

49. Ryan, *Juridical Effects*, 94–95.

"must be regarded as capable of giving access to that communion which is salvation."[50]

For Rahner, especially in the *Vorfragen*, this insight pushes him to consider the canonical questions anew. Instead of beginning from the canonical judgment and then inferring an answer to the question of grace, he argues that canon law describes the church's God-given being; it does not determine it. Therefore, attending *first* to what God is doing, especially in difficult cases, must affect how we make legal judgments. One of the sections in the *Vorfragen* is titled "Law as the Recognition of an Already Existing Reality."[51] He is clear that he is not arguing for a change in the canons as they are applied within the Roman Church. These canons exist appropriately and under the church's rightful authority. They define the normal case within the Roman Church. As the saying goes, "hard cases make bad law." The facts arising from the *surd* of ecclesial division need not change canon law. But precisely for this reason, canon law cannot be the church's only means for reasoning about God's work in the world.

Returning to marriage law, we can see how Rahner reorients the relationship of the canonical judgment to the existing reality: "It would seem that the case is simple: the earlier deficit in form had made the marriage (existentially and also socially) not actually invalid; the sanatio in radice merely recognizes explicitly that the lack of form that appeared to make the marriage impossible had not done so in this case. The lawgiver does not change the thing itself but redefines his own relationship to it. But from this we can

---

50. "Non paucae etiam christianae religionis actiones sacrae apud fratres a nobis seiunctos peraguntur, quae variis modis secundum diversam condicionem uniuscuiusque Ecclesiae vel Communitatis procul dubio vitam gratiae reapse generare possunt atque aptae dicendae sunt quae ingressum in salutis communionem pandant." *Unitatis redintegratio* §3 (translation mine).

51. See chapter 3. In this translation, this title has been simplified to "Recognizing Reality."

see that a single social status in the church can arise—or at least can be recognized as having arisen—from differing means."[52]

The canonical lawgiver is therefore not *providing* a sacramental reality to the couple now that must somehow be understood as moving backward into the past. Rather, he is restipulating his own understanding of God's work in the life of the couple, recognizing by his canonical decree that *God* has acted here and made the invalidly contracted marriage into one the church can recognize as valid. In this reframing, God remains the font of grace, even when the means are mysterious to the church. The church remains the ordinary conduit of sacramental grace, but does not seek to limit God's actions to its own.

Ordination and Ontology

Much is made of the category of "ontological change" in discussions of sacramental ordination.[53] And perhaps that, while not given explicit attention in the *Vorfragen*, provides a lens by which to summarize what has been said so far regarding Rahner's turning of the canonical field of view, prioritizing the church's role in discerning God's action rather than focusing on its own legal requirements.

---

52. See chapter 3.

53. The question of whether ordination produces an ontological change and, if so, in what it consists is a long-controverted one, especially between Catholics and Protestants. It is not my intention here to wade into that argument, although readers may find some ecumenical treatments of it helpful. In particular, the Lutheran-Catholic dialogue has made some interesting progress in understanding what is at stake in the question. Both Lutheran-Catholic and Anglican-Catholic dialogues tend to focus on the shared agreement that ordination is *unrepeatable* as a way to begin reframing the historically controverted question. See especially *Modern Ecumenical Documents*; ARCIC-I Final Report, *PCPCU Information Service* 49, nos. 2–3 (1982): 74–106, esp. 85; and US Conference of Catholic Bishops and Evangelical Lutheran Church in America, *Declaration on the Way: Church, Ministry and Eucharist* (Minneapolis: Augsburg Fortress, 2015), IV.B.3.

Throughout the *Vorfragen*, Rahner, while explicitly accepting the "official and scholastic teaching" of the church, sets his argument against the assumptions of a too-narrow scholasticism.[54] This scholasticism, as has been noted, tends to reason from cause to effect, taking the standard sacramental system as being simply equivalent with the outworking of God's grace in the world. We have seen above how this position and Rahner differ on interpreting the radical sanation of a marriage. But what might it mean for understanding the ordination of Protestant ministers—Rahner's chief area of concern?

Two ideas are key to his position. The first we have already discussed: the freedom of God to act in history, along with the church's resulting duty to look for the work of the Spirit. The second is the church's basic eschatological character. In the words of *Lumen gentium*, the church is a pilgrim people already, although mysteriously, in continuity with its final self in the kingdom of God.[55]

Holding these two notions together, the Roman Catholic Church, if it recognizes the work of the Spirit among the ordained ministries of Protestants, cannot help but relate them to the one eschatological church of Christ, which it understands to subsist in itself. Therefore, in the present, the remaining divisions among Christians can only be "borne spiritually on the way to unity."[56] Accepting the canonical judgment that Protestant ministries were invalid but seeing them now acting as means of grace, directed toward the one church of Christ, the church may find itself in a position analogous to the one it inhabits when it radically sanates a marriage. The church is recognizing a reality that has arisen by grace out of unusual, even sinful, beginnings.

This shifts the means by which ordination is understood within the Catholic framework in ways that are consistent with conciliar

---

54. See section 4.1.
55. *Lumen gentium*, chap. 7.
56. See chapter 6.

and postconciliar theologies. The traditional canonical framework encourages the theologian to consider ordination as a grace that an individual receives. Therefore, it becomes in some sense a thing that they possess. The *cursus honorem* by which a man proceeded through the minor orders toward priesthood came to be understood as an additive process by which grace could be measured as to "how much" one had received.[57] Grace is guaranteed by the rightly celebrated rite, which includes a properly ordained celebrant. This vision takes as its assumption that "under no circumstances could sacramental grace be construed as being conferred apart from a sacrament being conferred also."[58] Invalidity is thus taken to be a positive judgment of the nonexistence of grace rather than the negative judgment that the church's requirements for a sacrament have not been met.[59]

As was stated above, Rahner is deeply committed to the position that we discover the possible from the real.[60] This allows him to accept canonical judgments while giving precedence to an existential interpretation of the effects of those judgments over the traditional legal interpretations. If the church can recognize God operating outside of its boundaries, it must also recognize that from its own perspective, these actions are extraordinary. They are

---

57. An interesting analog is found in the argument about whether women can be ordained as deacons in the German-language literature. There, one of the arguments is whether the "unity of the sacrament of order" is to be understood as the unity of more and less of the same kind of thing, or another kind of unity. Theologians like K-H Menke argue that it must be the first and so "more grace" is conferred in later ordinations, requiring that anyone who is ordained to the diaconate must be able to be ordained to the episcopacy. I do not subscribe to this view; indeed, I believe it to force a misreading of *Lumen gentium* §29, as I have argued in "Female Deacons and the Unity of the Sacrament of Order: Responding to the German Skeptics," *Theological Studies* 82, no. 2 (June 2021): 351–70.

58. Ryan, *Juridical Effects*, 95; see also my own discussion above.

59. Rahner engages briefly with this question in chapter 6.

60. See my own discussion in footnote 27.

not covered by the law it has determined to describe its customary action. But it also cannot presume that its ideas about what is possible are more important than what it determines to exist in the world by God's extraordinary grace. Doing so would lead to an idolatry of the canonical-ecclesiastical system, confusing church practice with God. Because God is busy drawing all people to himself, Christians should be ever vigilant for the actions of grace beyond their usual borders. What determines what is possible, even if the canonical judgments are otherwise generally adequate descriptions of normal action within the boundaries of the visible, institutional church.

If the church reads its history backward from the reign of God, and canon law is taken to be the general description of the church's decisions about its life rather than as dispositive descriptions of the inner workings of grace, then Rahner's position also contributes to a different understanding of what ordination is and is for. It is still rightly described as imparting a sacramental character that can be understood as an ontological change. But that change is a change in the grace-driven relationship of the church to God. What is "ordered" is the church—individuals are given charisms for the upbuilding of the ecclesial body, especially in the roles of deacon, priest, and bishop.[61] These individuals are configured to Christ in his Body, the church, and therefore given particular roles (along with the grace to fulfill them). They become important parts of the structure—the Order—that God gives to the Body of Christ.

Encountering Christians separated from Rome, then, the first question is not "Is there a chain in history by which grace is passed down to these individuals?" but "How is God working in this community?" "Can the church judge that the form of the eschatological church is, by God's grace, present?" Importantly, this need not be an all-or-nothing, yes-or-no, valid-or-invalid choice. Instead, the

---

61. See Susan K. Wood, *Sacramental Orders* (Collegeville, MN: Liturgical Press, 2000), 22–23.

Catholic Church seeks to judge, as it begins to do in *Unitatis red-integratio*, to what extent the separated brethren are connected to the final church. It asks where there is grace such that the eschatological kingdom is visible and where there is not. Of course, the Roman Catholic Church must also ask these questions of itself. It asks them more fully in a conversation with other Christians that does not presume their total separation from God. In doing so, the church discerns the remaining distance on her pilgrimage in hope of God's mercy. In coming closer to Christ, it draws closer to all other Christians.

The Appendix on Intercommunion

This piece is appended to both the original printing of the *Vorfragen* and the version in the *Sämtliche Werke*. As Rahner states in the body of the main text, this article "came to be in a very different manner and has a very different purpose. It therefore uses an entirely different method" from the *Vorfragen*.[62] Specifically, Rahner wrote the excursus for the doctrinal commission of the German Bishops' Conference as they considered what rules should govern intercommunion.[63] Rahner saw the piece as serving this (divided) commission not by adding more suggestions to the pile but describing what would most likely constitute the consensus of the gathered bishops. In this, Rahner sees a difference in method between the *Vorfragen* and the appendix. While the first is maximalist in its questions, an expedition into the wild blue yonder in search of new questions and possibly a new way forward, the appendix is a sober reflection of the already-existing status quo at the service of formal rule-making.

Within the German churches, the question of whether and when intercommunion between Protestants and Catholics could be allowed was repeatedly being asked. To this day, Germany remains

---

62. See chapter 1.
63. See chapter 1, where Rahner describes this.

a source of this question, in part because of the frequency of inter-marriage between Christians of different confessions. The German bishops regularly push the whole church to consider how best to pastorally minister to these "mixed" marriages. In this piece, Rahner seeks to look at the Catholic guidelines at the time and discern what seemed to be nonnegotiable and what were questions of prudential judgment. The argument in this section is largely unrelated to the argument of the main text except for dealing with ecumenical questions. It is more sure and less speculative.

It is important to note two things about this section. First, here, Rahner considers under what circumstances non–Roman Catholic Christians can be admitted to the Eucharist celebrated by a Roman Catholic priest. It does not consider whether or when a Catholic could commune in another Christian community. Second, while he had briefly mentioned in the main text the possibility of joint celebrations of the Eucharist between Christians (see chapter 3), he does not consider such celebrations possible. One surprising aspect of the text is that Rahner does not directly engage with either the 1967 or 1972 directives from the Secretariat for Promoting Christian Unity on these questions.[64]

The appendix is structured in four sections.

Methodology
In this brief section, Rahner argues that the contemporary practice of the church, while not itself infallible, is nevertheless the appropriate starting point for considering norms for a practice-related question like intercommunion. Rahner outlines his method as analyzing the current norms, asking what principles arise from them, and finally asking whether norms for other situations can be derived from them.

---

64. For a clear summary and analysis of the Catholic development on these questions, see R. Kevin Seasotz, "One House, Many Dwellings, Open and Closed Communion," *Worship* 79 (2005): 405–19.

Initial Analysis of Extant Norms for Intercommunion
Considering the current practice of the Catholic Church regarding communing non-Catholic Christians, Rahner reduces them
to two norms: First, the rejection of "a general and unconditional admission of non-Catholic Christians . . . to full eucharistic
communion."[65] Second, there are cases where the church admits
non-Catholic Christians to the Eucharist despite the break in communion and the disagreements on church-dividing theological topics. The disjunct between the general prohibition and the specific
permission requires the discernment of the principles by which they
are made.

Principles Arising from These Norms
Rahner derives five principles from the application of the two
norms above. First, a legitimate intercommunion requires a certain
sameness of action in the Eucharist both objectively and, in a sense,
subjectively. Second, there is a difference between the private and
the communal symbolism of sacramental communion. Legitimate
intercommunion would have to be legitimated in both of these
realms. Third, answering whether a particular case of intercommunion may be justified at a personal level requires considering
reasons specific to the situation and asking whether in this case the
lack of visible communion with the Catholic Church is a matter
of indifferentism toward unity or an active rejection of it. Finally,
Rahner sums up, "Intercommunion, therefore, seems to be fundamentally forbidden only where it implies, in the public sphere, an
undeniable commitment to the fundamental equivalency of different confessions regarding the sacraments and the church," although
the consent of the church to the intercommunion is also necessary.[66]
This implies that the less public an act of intercommunion is, the

---

65. See appendix.
66. See appendix.

more likely it is that the church's ministers would be able to give permission.

Indications for Practical Norms

From these principles, Rahner derives five norms: First, that admission to the Eucharist presumes baptism, and that this requirement cannot be waived. Second, intercommunion does not allow the equal participation (i.e., a kind of concelebration) of ministers of separated confessions. Third, for the private communion of a non–Roman Catholic who does not specifically reject the Catholic Church, "a certain amount of generosity and tolerance seems to have a place."[67] A serious desire to participate may be honored even without a clear articulation of belief, given that many Catholics also cannot articulate the church's theology of the Eucharist or of communion clearly or accurately. Fourth, when it is unclear whether a person's lack of union with the church is "merely negative" or "positively privative," then the permission of church officials becomes more important.[68] Finally, as Rome has given explicit permission for some open communion, these cases provide further data for considering what situations might be understood as falling under the same kinds of permission.

Rahner's Development, 1974–84

Rahner lived for a decade after writing the *Vorfragen*, during which time he continued to engage with the questions he had begun to open up in this document. However, the *Vorfragen* remains his

---

67. See appendix.
68. See appendix. The difference here arises precisely because all contemporary Christians are born into a divided church. A Lutheran with ties of communion to Lutherans, therefore, has not necessarily made a positive decision to be out of communion with Rome. They may have, but they may also merely be living into the good bonds of communion with the family, community, and location into which they were born and baptized.

longest and most sustained engagement with them. In 1982, he explicitly returned to these with "Kleine Randbemerkung zur Frage des Amtsverständnisses" (A short marginal note on the understanding of ministry), first published in a Festschrift for Heinrich Fries.[69] He later revised and republished this work as "Zur Frage des Amtsverständnisses."[70] This work summarizes the thoughts he first developed in *Vorfragen*.

Rahner and Fries published their *Unity of the Churches: An Actual Possibility* in 1983. Rahner's work in the *Vorfragen* and "Kleine Randbemerkung" is neither directly cited nor referenced in this final book. However, the influence of the argument is discernable in theses 5 and 7. It is especially present in their consideration of the problem of insisting on an "unbroken succession" for validity.[71] This is essentially a reprisal of the argument made in *Vorfragen*.[72]

Rahner and Fries's argument for what makes an ordination valid despite this historical uncertainty and use of the analogy to the radical sanation of a marriage clearly develops Rahner's work in the *Vorfragen*.[73] They also specifically point to a question of retroaction of effects in thesis 7, although they do not directly explain what this means or how exactly Catholics could change their position regarding Protestant ministers:

> As has been said, and will be said again, the answer to the retroactive question of validity or non-validity of ministerial

---

69. F. P. Neuner and F. Wolfinger, eds., *Auf Wegen der Versöhnung* (Frankfurt: J. Knecht, 1982), 213–19.

70. Karl Rahner, "Zur Frage des Amtsverständnisses," in SW 27:215–19. The editing of the revised edition came to be in responding to comments from Roman censors on both parts through the addition of passages and parentheticals and the replacement of several compound words with hyphenated terms. It is translated by Joseph Donceel, SJ, as "Understanding the Priestly Office," in *TI*, 22:208–13.

71. Theses 5.3 and 7 in Fries and Rahner, *Unity of the Churches*, 99–101, 115–121.

72. See SW 27:246–48.

73. Fries and Rahner, *Unity of the Churches*, 120–21; cf. SW 27:248–50.

offices in the churches of the Reformation (from the perspective of Catholics today) is not something that would have to block the future unity of the churches, even if the answers are different. But in any case, this is valid for the future: the churches are challenged, in the documents mentioned above, to test anew the possibility of reestablishing the connection with the historical succession of the office of bishop as a sign of the unity of the faith.[74]

Rahner's questions in the *Vorfragen*, (1) how Catholics can recognize the work of the Spirit in the ministries of Protestant pastors and (2) how this changes the way that we talk about the history stemming from the Reformation, occupied him during the last decade of his life. He kept returning to them in different formats. Despite this long trajectory of engagement with the problem, however, it has remained an underconsidered aspect of his thought among scholars of Rahner's thought and ecumenists both.

New Questions: Protestant Ordination of Women

While some communities had begun ordaining women as pastors when Rahner originally wrote the *Vorfragen*, it was not the central concern of either the official dialogue at the time nor of the book. But this does not mean that Rahner's thesis does not have a bearing on the questions that have developed since he wrote. The ordination of women as pastors and as bishops has changed the ecumenical landscape and introduces not only a new question into the discussion but one that is freighted with more than just historical weight. Protestant communions that ordain women see this practice as a mandate of the gospel, the overcoming of an effect of the fall, and a way in which the kingdom is visibly breaking into the world and the church. Conversely, Catholic leaders have

74. Thesis 5.3 in Fries and Rahner, 101.

stated that the church is not empowered to ordain women as priests or bishops.[75]

This seems like another setting in which the question is a simple dichotomy. There is no intermediate position between "Yes, the church can ordain women as priests and bishops" and "No, it cannot." But while recognizing that this is a complex question that cannot be adequately answered in this brief space, and also remembering that Rahner himself does not provide an answer to this question, we can ask ourselves what his thought experiment might contribute to the contemporary ecumenical discussion.

Any adequate answer will need to balance the same two things that Rahner is attempting to hold in tension throughout the book: first, that the church is empowered to make binding decisions about its life that arise out of its understanding of the working out of the gospel in history, and second, that grace is a divine self-gift, made in history to particular people in particular places and times. We discover the possibility of grace from the actual playing out of grace in these places and times. When our understanding of what is possible is surprised by something "impossible" actually existing, it is our understanding, not the world, that must change.

And so the Catholic theologian, confronted with both their church's emphatic teaching through the contemporary era that women cannot be ordained to the presbyterate or the episcopate and also the existence of grace-filled Protestant ministries, must ask several questions. First, they must ask whether this teaching belongs to the infallible magisterial teaching of the church or not. This is a complex question. The Congregation for the Doctrine of the Faith has repeatedly declared that it belongs to the "ordinary universal magisterium"—that is, those teachings that the bishops of the

---

75. See footnote 11. The question of whether the Roman Catholic Church believes itself to be empowered to ordain women as permanent deacons is unanswered at this point. For a summary of some of the arguments and bibliography of the ongoing controversy, see my "Female Deacons."

world have consistently taught as necessary to the gospel without ever having juridically enacted.[76] But as Richard Gaillardetz pointed out, it is not clear that the Congregation for the Doctrine of the Faith itself has the authority to declare that something belongs to this category. In other words, the declaration by the Congregation for the Doctrine of the Faith that this teaching is infallible is not itself an infallible teaching.[77] Despite this difficulty, Rahner's tendency would be to give deference to the curial and papal reiteration of something as decided. Whether or not the teaching is infallible, it has been consistently reiterated by the last four popes, who have repeatedly declared it to be a closed question.[78]

But if they are to follow Rahner's lead, our contemporary Catholic theologian will also have to consider that they are confronted with Protestant brothers and sisters who receive sacramental signs and hear the word preached by women their communities understand to be priests and bishops. How is this phenomenon to

76. Congregation for the Doctrine of the Faith, "Responsum Ad Propositum Dubium concerning the Teaching Contained in *Ordinatio sacerdotalis*," October 28, 1995, https://www.vatican.va/roman_curia/congregations/cfaith/documents/rc_con_cfaith_doc_19951028_dubium-ordinatio-sac_en.html; and Cardinal Luis F. Ladaria, Si, "In Response to Certain Doubts regarding the Definitive Character of the Doctrine of *Ordinatio sacerdotalis*," Congregation for the Doctrine of the Faith, accessed January 21, 2022, https://www.vatican.va/roman_curia/congregations/cfaith/ladaria-ferrer/documents/rc_con_cfaith_doc_20180529_caratteredefinitivo-ordinatiosacerdotalis_en.html.
77. Richard R. Gaillardetz, "Infallibility and the Ordination of Women," *Louvain Studies* 21 (1996): 3–24, https://richardgaillardetz.files.wordpress.com/2014/04/infallibility_and_the_ordination_of_women.pdf.
78. Pope Paul VI, "Response to the Letter of His Grace the Most Reverend Dr. F. D. Coggan, Archbishop of Canterbury, concerning the Ordination of Women to the Priesthood," November 30, 1975, Acta Sanctae Sedis 68 (1976), 599; Pope John Paul II, *Ordinatio sacerdotalis*. Benedict XVI authored several responses as president of the Congregation of the Doctrine of the Faith, and Francis treated the matter briefly. Pope Francis, *Evangelii Gaudium*, Apostolic Exhortation, November 24, 2013, §§103–4.

be understood? At the very least, the theologian must attempt to discern the possible from the real and take the experience of grace in these communities seriously.

Rahner begins the *Vorfragen* with a thought experiment of several lay Christians finding themselves trapped in Siberia. He asks whether God would deprive them of the grace of the Eucharist if they were to gather to celebrate it. Neither the thought experiment nor the answer is dependent on the gender of our hypothetical Siberians. If God would not deny the grace of the sacrament, the *res tantum* of the Eucharist to this group of the faithful who find themselves isolated from the institutional church, this must be part of our consideration.

But how can this be squared with Rahner's commitment to take the magisterial teaching of the church seriously? I cannot answer for Rahner. But his proposal that we can recognize legitimate sacraments without regular officeholders is interesting, and might change the seemingly zero-sum game of the contemporary dialogue. If the Roman Church is able to recognize that grace is present in the eucharistic gatherings of contemporary Protestants, then it should *at least* recognize that the women ordained in these communities are something analogous to priests and bishops, even if it still believes that the Roman Church is incapable of ordaining women. This recognition would seem to be borne out in papal practice. The same popes who have repeatedly declared the Catholic Church *unable* to ordain women to the priesthood have welcomed Lutheran and Anglican women *as leaders of their own communions*. Pope Francis, for example, traveled to Lund, Sweden, to commemorate the five hundredth anniversary of the Reformation. At this event, Pope Francis prayed with the female archbishop of Uppsala, Antje Jackelén, and gave her the sign of peace as leader of her community. Moreover, when Joseph Ratzinger wrote to the Lutheran bishop Hanselmann claiming that "validity" was the wrong category for the Lutheran Eucharist, because the Catholic Church recognizes that Eucharist as capable of giving access to the communion with

God that is salvation, he was describing a communion with female pastors and bishops and was therefore also describing their eucharistic celebrations.

If we are committed to discerning the work of God in the world, finding the Spirt where it is moving, then Rahner must say that these Protestant communities also participate eschatologically in the future of the one, holy, catholic and apostolic church. As Rahner sums up, "The best way to say it is this: the effectiveness of the sacraments (and, let us add, *mutatis mutandis*, the legitimacy of office) is ultimately the effectiveness of the 'sign' as such."[79] In other words, if we discern that the sign of the archbishop of Uppsala is effective by the grace of God, then there is a legitimacy to her office, because it participates in God's final desire for the church. The church cannot merely say, "This is impossible and so it does not exist." It must also be honest about discovering the stirrings of the Spirit in places it would not have anticipated.

This, of course, does not provide a complete answer for how a Catholic theologian will respond to the Protestant female bishop or pastor nor to the calls for the ordination of women by the Catholic Church. If Rahner does not finally provide an answer to our contemporary question, we should not be surprised. Not only was it not among his own, but he sees the text of the *Vorfragen* itself as preliminary and in need of more development. As Rahner concludes in chapter 5 (which was originally the end of the whole piece), "It should not be asserted that any particular act in any Christian denomination that has any affinity with the Catholic sacraments should necessarily be recognized as a sacrament or that any permanent function in any Christian denomination is already a ministry within the meaning of order transmitted in the Catholic Church through a sacramental ordination. Here I have only asked questions, and very general ones at that. But one *is* still permitted to ask."

---

79. See chapter 6.

Catholics cannot and should not deny that God is working—and working richly—among Protestant communities, including those led by women. The task of ecumenical engagement in such a situation is to listen to one's own community, to the experience of the other, and for the movement of the Spirit in the world. The beauty of following the path of Rahner's thought experiment is that in doing so, we open up our eyes to practice looking for the Spirit's action. That Spirit draws all separated Christians toward a single fulfillment in which the one, final Body of Christ is made whole. God's redemption of the sin that is the basis of every division draws us to unexpected places, bringing forth new realities that we can only glimpse for now. But standing together, we can practice looking to the present for hints of what is to come.

Conclusion

Rahner's thought experiment in the *Vorfragen* is certainly not the final word on the question of Rome's recognition of Protestant ministers. It is not even Rahner's final word. But the lack of attention that this slim volume has received in the English-language conversation is nevertheless surprising. Here is a careful beginning to a question that has only become more vexing in ecumenical dialogue since 1973. In the wake of the *Joint Declaration on the Doctrine of Justification* and the ever-widening reception that that document has received in Protestant communions, the ecumenical relationships of the Roman Catholic Church have become more and more vexed by the question of ecclesiology. For Roman Catholic thinkers, ecclesiality cannot be divorced from the question of valid ministers.[80] But Roman Catholics also cannot allow invalidity to be our only word on these questions. To do so is to ignore the Second Vatican

---

80. The Congregation for the Doctrine of the Faith has repeatedly made this point. See Congregation for the Doctrine of the Faith, "Communionis notio," §§17–18.

Council, the writings and behaviors of contemporary popes, and the Spirit of God in the world.

I do not believe that this document answers all questions, nor did Rahner. But it is my hope that this translation of Rahner's *Vorfragen* might give this work a hearing among English-language theologians that it has not received so far. Perhaps Rahner's suggestions and thought experiments will offer a neglected point of entry into our current questions about ecclesiality, ordination, and the nature of the church.

Foreword

The humble intention and the limits of the deliberations of this little *quaestio disputata* will be spelled out in the first section of this volume. It directly and explicitly wades into the academic controversies that have recently arisen about the possibility of a mutual recognition of ministries[1] among the separated churches. I will only propose certain considerations that impinge on the edges of this controversy here and raise my own consciousness about a problem of which I myself was not previously aware. These considerations, which produce more aporias than answers and will be engaged with relatively little erudition, will inevitably tend toward the speculative. If the reader were to also come to this conclusion, I could not possibly receive it as a rebuke or a criticism. My thanks to Fr. Harald Schöndorf for his help.

Karl Rahner, SJ
Munich, February 1974

---

1. *Ämter*. I will generally be translating *Amt* as "ministry" or "order" depending on context, although "office" would be a more exact translation. This is to follow the usual usage in English-language theology.

1

Asking the Question,
Imagining an Answer

This volume not only appears in the series called Quaestiones Disputatae; it is also truly a *quaestio disputata*. It intends to consider an open question, not to report a settled view. It means to describe an argument within an open theological disputation that is not yet closed but must be pushed further. Better, it intends to ask questions and register thoughts about them that will require further consideration in order to clarify the matter about which they ask. This matter turns out to be not so clear after all and will require much more work, for so much important theological data, so many facts and possibilities, require reconsideration and application in this context. And so I do not wish to offer a complete solution. This volume is, in a strong sense, a response to a disputed question, as naturally the book of a single theologian will always inevitably be.

The occasion of this work is the work of the Evangelical and Catholic Ecumenical Institutes of Germany.[a] It appears to this author that the answer given by the doctrinal commission of the German Bishops' conference to that work[b] is either too quick to judge according to a very particular manner, or at least seems to do so to this reader. The desire to quickly produce a magisterial clarification can in fact cheapen the respect that is owed to such pronouncements. However, the book of the above-named institutes is not the subject of this little *quaestio disputata* and will not approach the "ordination question" in the same manner as that book did. Can the contemporary major churches mutually recognize their ministries and the manner of their exercise? This is the question with which the institutes' book and the contrary *Clarification* dealt.[1] Admittedly, this publication will also relate to that question.

This volume is intentionally conceived as an exercise in blue-skying.[2] It was discussed with many people from many directions. The basic theme was contemplated from the most divergent positions possible. These various points of view and starting points and their respective considerations have not been strongly systematized. More is asked than answered. The volume should never lose this character in the reader's understanding, especially in attempting at the end to find hidden answers in the open questions themselves (should they produce such) and thus derive a system from them. Whoever would refuse from the beginning to undertake such a speculative journey should ask themselves if there, at the source of any truly original theology driven by creative forces (even should one possesses a staff, with which one can navigate the fog[3]), one will not always find such a speculative attempt standing at the *beginning* of each theological consideration. Isn't this actually inevitable, if one is not merely going to be reciting and defending completed and already-proven theological theses? Naturally, such theological considerations are usually only employed in quiet alone. Only *afterward* is the completed idea first constructed in a strong systematic sense and a proof attempted. But why shouldn't one occasionally

---

1. Rahner here refers to the 1973 German memorandum *Reform und Anerkennung kirchlicher Ämter: Ein Memorandum der Arbeitsgemeinschaft ökumenischer Universitätsinstitute*.
2. Here, as in the foreword, Rahner calls the project *eine Fahrt ins Blaue*—literally, "a trip off into the blue" (as in the wild blue yonder).
3. Rahner here refers to the saying "mit dem Stange im Nebel stochern"—that is, "to poke around in the fog with a stick."

demonstrate one's own attempts to come to conclusions, or even allow a window into the theological workshop? Why shouldn't one occasionally print such a "worker's monologue," even if the tentative character of it is clear? Is the attempt to jump over a ditch only interesting once the jumper has cleared the trench and we can be certain that he will not fall into it?

In such an attempt, which appears to this author to be permitted, it is self-evident that the critical apparatus of theological argumentation may also be lacking. People (e.g., Hans Küng°) have already implied that I am a despiser of historical theology (both in the exegetical sense and also in the history of dogmas); I supposedly would prefer to jump straight to speculation. But I feel myself to be accused unjustly in this manner because I am not of the opinion that what one might dismiss as theological speculation is the only legitimate theological method. It is certainly not. But regarding historical work, if it does not wish it to become barren, it should not weave the illusion around itself of not having *questions* that cannot be explained by the historical material alone. If one has no questions, the historical theological material remains silent, and one remains blind viewing it.

But where do the questions for the advancement of theology come from, without which historical investigation, including the study of magisterial pronouncements, remains dumb and blind? From a double but unified source: first, from the life of the church in the present, its needs and requirements and the relationship of the churches among themselves; and second from the tensions that exist—half sensed, half unconsidered—between the individual moments of life, the praxis of the church, and the normal ruling scholastic theology. Such things must be clarified first by an initial reflection and raised into consciousness. In this way, questions and aporias arise, only after which can one turn to the proper theological "sources" (in the conventional sense). Such a first level of reflection, as one could name this initial search (even if it is found already mixed into every truly theological work), does not demand a complex scientific apparatus. One can appeal to facts and teachings that are commonly known. If one wished to scientifically "prove" such appeals at great length, one could spread the haze of a great theological erudition all around such a consideration. But such erudition does not have many actual uses. One can confidently leave such work to dissertations and theses.

The appendix concerning "open communion" that is attached to this work came to be in a very different manner and has a very different purpose. It therefore uses an entirely different method, about which the beginning of that article provides enough information. This article arose as a paper composed for the doctrinal commission of the German bishops' conference, when it occupied itself with the question of "intercommunion." Admittedly, it progressed little beyond the conclusion that, within the committee itself, very different opinions held sway. The occasion and the goal of this paper entailed that the committee did not desire more suggestions, as if its author intended to say that he hoped for the possibility of a consensus among the commission and expected to be able to achieve one, especially if such a hope could ultimately not be fulfilled. The charge for this paper therefore required considerably more constrained limits than those of these considerations framed as a *quaestio disputata*. That paper sought, in my opinion and from my point of view, a kind of "minimal program," even if it was too far-reaching for some members of the above-referenced commission. This work here, as an actual *quaestio disputata*, aims at something more in the direction of a maximal program. If this difference, of which the author himself is quite aware, is attended to, the reader will not misunderstand how the two works contained in this volume can fit together. It is especially important on this question because the report regarding open communion only deals with the question of under what circumstances a Protestant Christian can be allowed to receive at a Catholic celebration of the Eucharist; the opposite question is never actually asked. The present work, however, asks precisely this question: How could or can one understand a contemporary Protestant Eucharist theologically from a Catholic perspective (if this be truly Catholic and not legalistically narrowed), even though this question requires in turn that the essay itself adopt the more global perspective of "ministry" generally?

In order to correctly evaluate this *quaestio disputata*, the following must also be stressed: This work proceeds from the assumption that the church *can do* (and perhaps in the actual "economy" *does*) much more in the realm of sacraments and ministry than her scholastic theology reflects or explicitly knows to be true. This also means that the question of possibilities and that of practical realities (whether when implicitly, or especially when explicitly, determined by the church itself) must be distinguished. Making this important distinction means that it is not certain that the realm of the real is simply identical to the realm of that which is explicitly sacramentally and canonically permitted. To the contrary, it is precisely the intent of this work to make possible a conception of the sacramental realm, through an "economical" validation, that is not simply identical with the realm of things recognized as valid by sacramental canon law. However, although the distinction in question remains fundamentally valid, there can be things that are sacramentally invalid *because* the church does not recognize them. But above all, because it cannot be inferred that the thesis of a validity by "economy" is simply certain, this means that in the entirety of this theological work, there will be no independently practicable norm for Catholics as to how to judge non-Catholic ministers and sacramental practice. The question of practical norms (at least according to my intention) receives only a preparatory study in the present work, no more. Many will judge this to be inadequate. I disagree. One can employ an ecclesial pragmatism as the impulse for theological considerations and their practical conclusions. Such a pragmatism does not replace the theological consideration itself. And such theological work must begin with preparatory considerations. With this caveat, the question must remain open as to how far a single person, according to the usual ethical rules, can practically apply such uncertain precepts in cases where there is no offense (i.e., no basic contempt for the explicit canonical norms) and make use in practice of these considerations that are being presented here for investigation.

One other limit of this work ought to be made explicit at this point—that is, regarding its genre.[4] Ministry and sacraments are generically spoken of throughout. This work will speak regarding ministry in general and sacraments in general (even when examples are provided) and will consider both terms together and singly. This appears to the author to be justified by the very nature of an *initial* consideration. But naturally, it is clear that this effect, to the extent that it is true, remains very general and not directly applicable to any particular problem. Different ministries must be distinguished from one another, and the ministries of specific churches ought to be distinguished and are understood in the different churches to be differentiated; the sacraments are also differentiable and are differentiated within the different churches in their existence and practice. So one must be careful within such a general consideration about drawing immediate conclusions about any particular ministry in a church or any particular sacrament. The present work makes no such assertions. If, however, the present work only manages to show that according to the facts and data of Catholic teaching and praxis, its supposition that a clear concept of *economy* is conceivable and that concept allows the recognition of sacraments and ministries in the other Christian churches beyond what is already recognized (perhaps by using the term *economy* itself), then this study has fulfilled its purpose.

---

4. Rahner uses the term *genus literarium*.

2

The Essence of the Church's Structure

1. Initial Considerations

A short story to start. Many years ago, one of the most important Protestant theologians in Germany said to me, "Imagine, if
you will, a pair of Christians is banished to Siberia and lives there
alone and without an ordained priest (according to their beliefs).
And now, tell me, can these people really not celebrate the Lord's
Supper with each other? Do you really believe that God would say
in this case, 'You poor, lonely Christians abandoned by the entire
world, who must *truly* take part in my Son's passion in a most bit-
ter manner, I'm very sorry, but I cannot help you, for there is a law
iuris divini (of divine law) according to which the Lord's Supper can
only be celebrated with an ordained priest as celebrant; I can't do
anything about this. I will bless you in other ways and help you, but
I'm sorry, there can be no celebration of the Eucharist for you.' Is
this not (so asked the theologian) a specifically Catholic God, or a
rabbinic God, who has the law on his knee, reads it, and interprets
it strictly? Is this not legalism, the opposite of the gospel?" This is
approximately what this theologian said.[a]

I felt rather cornered. This is something unusual for the theologian. I don't quite know anymore how I answered him then. But I
probably said something like this: "My dear colleague, there is an

old and simple distinction, which one also cannot entirely avoid in Protestant theology—that is, the distinction between the dimension of the sacramental sign and the dimension of the grace of God expressed and made present through the sacramental sign. If you accept, for example, which is indeed more difficult for you than me, that an unbaptized person might also be justified, then in practice you are also making this distinction. And neither of us would deny the meaning or the necessity of the sacraments because such an extrasacramental grace occurs, just as Peter knew that Cornelius already had the Spirit but baptized him nonetheless. Accordingly, my honored colleague, one must distinguish between the conditions that make an operation in the realm of the sacraments legitimate (you would not baptize with sand if you found yourself in the desert without water, or even if you did, you would repeat it with water as soon as possible) and the conditions under which grace itself, which is normally given with and by the sacrament, comes to be, even under circumstances where the legitimate sacramental sign is lacking. These two conditions are not of the same type, and so it is possible that the first could be lacking and the second present. Thus, the grace of the sacraments (the *res sacramenti*) is present.

"And this is precisely what the Council of Trent, about which you are so suspicious, knows to be true about the Eucharist.[b] It recognizes a 'spiritual communion' (there is an entire book about this by H. R. Schlette[c]). According to this, one does not merely ineffectively wish when one desires to receive the Body of Christ. Instead, one receives those pneumatic effects of the inner union with the ascended Lord, for which the bodily reception of the consecrated bread is only the sign. And so it is not really so upsetting, from either the divine or human viewpoint, when your people off in Siberia produce no valid sacramental signs. That very thing which is to be represented and made present in the sign, this comes about and is truly received by these Siberians. And this is not the excuse of a contemporary liberal Catholic theologian but is the opinion of the Council of Trent, in line with the older patristic tradition. And this is of course self-evident, for one (even a Catholic, despite your opinion) does *not* allow God to be a God who must always and in each case regulate himself by his law."—I probably said something like this and certainly had the impression then that I had successfully harmonized Catholic principles with a nonlegalist conception of God.

In the meantime, however, I have become (according to my own opinion) somewhat more clever, or perhaps (according to the opinion of a more "orthodox" type) somewhat stupider. Today I think this: my answer was entirely sensible for considering how an unbaptized person[1] is justified through faith, hope, and love alone and then through a "spiritual communion" celebrates the eucharistic union with his Lord. But for those Siberians, something quite different is going on: here we have baptized Christians who live out their lives in a situation in which an explicit Christian faith, the Scriptures, and a dependency on the church as the Body of Christ as a historically concrete social reality pertain; they speak the words of the commemoration of the Lord's death, they have a communal celebration in prayer and Christian love, and so they—definitely—receive the *res sacramenti* of the Eucharist. Also, what they do in their celebration has a connection to this *res sacramenti*, and this *res sacramenti* has a connection to the concrete ecclesial sign-character that they enact and *therefore* to these Siberians, who are the church in this place (at least to the extent that a house church of the New Testament was). And so I ask myself, Where is the remaining difference between this and a valid eucharistic celebration? One can, of course, still say that the *sign* of the grace-filled reality is not in a strong *sacramental* sense valid; perhaps an "orthodox" theologian would say that there is a sign there but that this works only *ex opere operantis*, not *ex opere operato*. But then one should ask what this distinction truly and really means in *this* case, when that which happens here symbolically happens within the

---

1. Literally, "ein Heide ungetauft"—that is, "an unbaptized heathen."

church, whose eschatologically victorious and irreversible reality is itself a sign that through them and in them is concluded by a final commitment—this sign of that which communicates what is meant by the dark words *opus operatum* and is even bound up in the subjective "intention" of the sacramental act[2] and with the faith, hope, and love of those receiving the sacrament? Why is this Siberian sign no real *opus operatum* when it is indeed located in the church according to the will of Christ? If this concrete celebration is the event through which and under which the "spiritual communion" of these people happens, so as to make present the *res sacramenti*, why may I not say that this sign makes present this *res sacramenti*? Are these words of the eucharistic thanksgiving not effective[3]? Why not? And if someone says, "Yes, these ritual words bring about the pneumatic unity with the risen Lord, but not his specific 'Real Presence,' as it is made present in a valid eucharistic celebration," then one must say that this Real Presence is itself only important and meaningful *insofar* as it brings about a pneumatic unity with Christ (and this only in the realm of the sign, not as the *res sacramenti* itself). Without this reference and this effect, the Real Presence itself would be no more than when, for example, a Judas sits next to the Lord at the Last Supper. But when the greater has come to pass, why shouldn't here and under *these* concrete conditions the smaller of the signs, the Real Presence, also occur? Because the required conditions of the (admittedly) lesser signs are missing? But how does someone know that in *this* case so certainly and exactly? Does it not assume something that must itself first be proved—that is, that in *all* conceivable situations, even extreme cases, *every* condition that in normal cases quite rightly applies for the constitution of the validity of the sign is still necessarily required? If someone wants to name as sacraments only those things that fulfill these requirements under normal circumstances and under normal legal jurisdiction,

---

2. *Sakramentensetzung.*
3. Literally, "exhibitive."

that is quite right; go with God. But in what are the two signs distinguished in any particular case? To this question, no one can give me any other tangible answer than this: that the Siberian sign must naturally be in accordance with the intention that is necessary to access the one true Supper under normal circumstances in commemorating the death of the Lord and corresponding to the intention of the church (which may be understood as the intention of Christ)—that is, it is one [presided over by] an ordained priest—and that, were this intention not present, the attitude of the celebrants would not be proper. Can anyone point to a real difference—without resorting to a war over terms—between these two, when in both situations truly both the sign of the reality and the reality itself are present?

What's more, one ought not forget that the "physical" presence, which one would only admit to be present in a normal consecration by an ordained priest, also belongs to the realm of the sign. Therefore, in the realm of the sign, not absolutely every difference must be denied. But it is not a difference that removes the sacramental reality, the *res sacramenti*, from *either* situation. And a difference, that truly—when one does not try to be overpicky about words out of a sense of clerical obstinacy—only consists of the fact that the one sign represents the *normal* (sensible) ecclesial case and the other an extraordinary, but nevertheless divinely decreed, intention that is included within the normal case and makes present the *res sacramenti*. Would one be able to make an ordinary Christian person understand that there is more of a difference? Would they be able to distinguish *opus operantis* from *opus operatum*—let alone spiritual communion under the truly Christian and ecclesial sign present here, from which only the word *sacrament* is withheld—and would they be able to value it and put it into effect?[4] I believe not. Is, moreover,

_____

4. The distinction between *opus operantis* and *opus operatum* arises in the argument over Donatism. They distinguish the contribution of the sacramental action (*opus operatum*) from that of the participant (*opus operantis*). The terms became controversial

that thing on which the theologians insist in order to defend the
normal ecclesial form as compulsory, but which a normal Christian
cannot grasp, so important that one must deny the word *sacrament* to
that Siberian celebration of the Eucharist, whose sense and meaning one must clearly admit? Must one do this only to underline the
difference between the two signs, which no one would deny or even
desire to deny? If we did deny it, would we not therefore be accepting that the God who willed the one incarnate, historical, worded,
communal order of effective grace, and not a world without [such]
grace, would trip up over his own laws, which he desires for *us* and
not for himself? And this is the main issue around which this question (and nothing more) revolves: Should one not think about why
and how such a sign in an extraordinary case (which might be extraordinary, naturally, in a number of different ways) could obtain
its sacramental dignity and power? This is the matter to which the
following will attend, after we have told just one more short story.

There are several considerations that should be made clearer
here about the contemporary controversy that is raging about the
possibility of a common recognition of ministries among the larger
Christian churches.[5] This controversy that has arisen on account of
the book of the Ecumenical Institutes of the German Universities
about the ministries of the church and the contrary *Declaration* published by the Doctrinal Commission of the German Bishops' Conference can be assumed to be generally well known in this work.[6] It
is not the task of this work to lay out the points of argument here

---

once again in the Protestant reformation, where Luther in particular saw many
applications of *ex opere operatum* in theology as potentially reducing the sacraments
to magic. See Paul C. Empie and T. Austin Murphy, eds., *Lutherans and Catholics in
Dialogue*, vol. 3, *The Eucharist as Sacrifice* (Minneapolis: Fortress, 1967).
5. He refers throughout to "den großen Christlichen Kirchen." In Rahner's setting, this refers to the EKD, the Evangelical Church of Germany, and the Catholic
Church. The nature of his consideration, however, remains general and is not
directly tied to these particular communions and the specificities of their ministries.
6. See the critical introduction to this volume.

or to focus explicitly on the questions of dispute and test the arguments of the two sides so as to attempt to settle the controversy once and for all. If this were the intention of the work, much more historical material and a survey of ecclesial-magisterial texts would have to be dealt with than can justly be engaged in such a slim and humble volume as this. But because each may choose his own subject according to his own pleasure, several relatively harmless considerations will be attempted that may perhaps be able to produce a certain loosening up of habitual manners of thought, at least among defenders of the "more rigorist" opinion in this controversy (but certainly not only among them), as these appear in or (by a more cautious interpretation) affect the most recent declaration of the Congregation for the Doctrine of the Faith, "Mysterium ecclesiae" of June 24, 1973.[d]

If one considers the very terse *Declaration* of the German doctrinal commission, it appears that their rejection of the book of the Ecumenical Institute is grounded in a double reference: First, that regarding the juridical constitution of the church and especially the structure of ministries and how they were conferred in the time of the New Testament, we know with far too little exactitude to draw absolutely certain theological conclusions about the contemporary question. Second, and reversed, in the book of the Ecumenical Institute, the later explicit and unambiguous convictions of the Roman Catholic Church about ministries (and the constitution of the church in general) are given short shrift, and because of the lack of attention given to these convictions—and this is openly stated—the theory of the book is simply rejected. Now, one can allow such an official declaration the right to be short and to leave elaboration and more specificity to theologians. But even under these conditions, one might still believe that this Declaration is too short and too simple. One might have the impression that it proceeds far too easily from the (real or putative) contemporary theological situation and simply takes this as absolutely dogmatically binding. On *this* basis, then, the Declaration takes the vagueness of the New

Testament regarding the understanding of ministry as simple and unproblematic permission to hold itself as decided on the contemporary theological situation without asking if this uncertainty and vagueness in the New Testament and the apostolic era might itself have a positive meaning. The question, therefore, is never raised in the face of this theological positivism as to *how* one might have considered the original revelation of the teaching, which one regards to be binding from the contemporary understanding of the faith (real or supposed)—a question to be asked and answered by theologians under the assumption that the contemporarily extant and developed understanding of the faith is itself binding. This question, however, is clearly not easy to answer in our case, because the Declaration of the commission itself posited a considerable uncertainty regarding the New Testament. In the search after an answer to the question, one ought not move too quickly or easily to the assumption that the church's teaching office can more easily uncover the right answer in these unclear and ambiguous sources than the historical theologian, or indeed that it has already discovered it clearly and completely.

The considerations so far have no other intention than to begin to reach out into a dark area to which scholastic theology, which perhaps speaks somewhat too surely in the Declaration of the doctrinal commission, does not pay enough notice. Particular theses will not be set up and defended. And so, in those areas where it does attend, and to which it listens, the single goal of these pages is to contribute a small amount to the differentiation and clarification of the state of the question, a state such that (at this point) in this question, no progress and no union of the churches can be hoped for.

It can be candidly and truly admitted that this author is of the opinion (which does not mean the clear, unchangeable conviction) that, in the field in question, there is *much* that does not simply exist according to the will of God and Christ, and *therefore* is established and recognized by the church as proceeding from the dimension of the self-realization of the church itself. These things are as they are because the church determined them, partly as a consequence of its own being, partly determined by the church's free decision. Such things can either be revised again later or (without prejudice to the earlier freedom of choice) determined to be irreversible, because they were decided in the apostolic era (the era of ongoing revelation), and remain valid for all later times.

The opinion that much of the teaching on ministry and on sacraments that is defined by the church as valid and permanent was not *defined* as such because it *is* such but because it was defined as such in a legitimate *settlement*[7] (in an entangled unity of theory and praxis, in which the praxis is not *merely* the execution of the theory) will not be proved here in a strong argument. On the contrary, consideration should be given to such a possible "proof" that could clarify and sharpen the consciousness of the problem in this whole question so that perhaps at a later time, the basic opinion just hinted at here can be "proven," for which, of course, more exact biblical and dogmatic-historical studies would be necessary.

Here, it seems, the path goes off into the theological "wild blue yonder." But that does not hurt anything. It can in this way clarify that even for a Catholic theologian, the field for possible maneuvers is much greater in this question of ministry than one is accustomed to think. According to these intentions, it is understandable that the considerations will begin from the most divergent starting points and their convergence will only slowly become clear. As has been said, this project will begin from conventional Catholic ecclesiology. Because of this, it will presuppose and stipulate many things that may seem cumbersome, far-fetched, and even downright sophistical to a Protestant theologian. They might form the impression that the question that is actually and ultimately scoped out could be defined, attained, and answered much more simply and directly—especially if they begin from the assumptions that are their own and that they affirm. But a Protestant theologian should also not overlook the

---

7. *Setzung.*

fact that when an ecumenical bridge is to be built, each must begin building from *their own* point of origin if it is to be hoped that the official church will one day accept the bridge that will be built. Theological changes in consciousness are made possible not when a new consciousness is decreed to be self-evident but rather when they begin from the official or scholastic consciousness and build based on their own intrinsic approaches to seek to make such changes as needed. This is most of all true in the church, for whom a historical continuity of consciousness is required by her very nature.

2. Where the Juridical Account of the Church Fails

I still remember sitting in a consultation of the theological commission in Rome during the council among learned bishops and theologians.[e] We were discussing the proposition that the College of Bishops exists with and under the pope and so is capable of action only in concert with him. All legal action in the church that wishes to be valid would explicitly or implicitly be bound to this precondition. In every single case. Now if the College of Bishops, which is indeed the highest legal entity in the church, only has this juridical authority in connection with the pope, then this is also true of every other bearer of juridical authority in the church, at least regarding the exercise of such juridical authority.

Regarding this proposition, I thought to myself, How is this actually true for those instances of law that are based in one or more of the sacraments but are instituted by someone who does not stand under the pope but desires to or that are administered during the *sede vacante*? In the first case, I had no answer if an explicit or implicit authorization of a juridical act on the part of the pope is always necessary and can only come from him. This first problem has certainly not been eliminated if one naively and simply assumes that according to the will of God, many administrations of the sacraments, even those meeting the necessary conditions, do not receive even the implicit authorization on the part of the pope but are nonetheless valid. Then the principle of a universal dependency on the pope for all legal actions within the church is repudiated. If one wants to support the principle by positing that the pope explicitly or implicitly gives authorization also to heretics and schismatics, then one must ask how such a thing might be possible. Or one might ask, so as to delve the matter more intentionally, whether such a grant of authority to heretics or schismatics is unthinkable and even if their juridical act in the administration of the sacraments is nevertheless valid. We would have to begin considering this question with the case of the validity of absolution by Orthodox priests, which none of us deny any longer. But one can certainly have doubts about whether this path has already led to a clear and simple outcome on the basis of the typical scholastic theology.

The reception (even of a child) into the true church by means of the baptism by a heretic is, even if implicitly, a fundamentally juridical act. Already by the time of Cyprian, the question of how a heretic might be capable of such an act was being asked.[f] Even up to the present, it seems to me, this is not understood in light of the usual assumptions. And so on this point, one might ask, Is there something in the objective church, from whose (necessary!) structure (to ask about its legitimacy!) individual offices precede and thus that legitimizes legal acts under certain circumstances—even if the one who establishes these acts, if measured only by the explicit structure of offices and its needs, is not in himself capable of doing so? How else should one explain that a heretic can validly baptize? Should one posit a positive revelation in the time of the apostles as to its validity? Cyprian already contests that this is the case, and it would seem that he was right. So how can one explain this validity? Mustn't the celebrant of a valid baptism-by-heretic indeed stand in some sort of positive connection to that legally established and mediated original reality, into which they are incorporating [someone] by their dispensing of baptism, and this even though they are not allowed "in themselves" to baptize? "In themselves" is here understood in relation to those structures of office that the church considers to be necessary to this original reality.

For the second case (sacramental administration as a juridical act during the *sede vacante*), I asked myself, Is such administration of the sacraments possible because of the continuing validity of a juridical provision (whether explicit or implicit) of the deceased pope? But what existential-ontological and ecclesiological assumptions must be made in this case, such that the will of a pope still legally exists and is binding after his death? Is this already explained by the theory that laws in a society are valid, and must be valid, even when the physical person who made them is no longer among the living? Does this information not, at its most basic, imply the existence of a law-giving or (if one wishes) law-bearing society that is still present when the physical person who normally effects and bears such law-giving is not present at the moment? How must one then think of the church, if one wishes to affirm this latter question? If there must be such a law-giving and law-bearing being in the church in order to answer this question, then it is not possible that such a church can effect "paracanonical" law in the cases where the sensible and necessary explicit law no longer suffices. And again, I no longer had a clear answer to my question.

At the meeting, however, I said only this (in part because I had not come to a satisfactory conclusion in my own considerations): OK, but there is indeed *one* highest, most significant juridical act in the church, one that creates new legal relationships and yet is not dependent on the explicit or implicit consent of the pope: that is, the choice of a new pope. I do not remember hearing in the commission's meeting a clarifying explanation to this harmless statement. I noticed only that G. Philips, the leading man of the commission, was fairly taken aback. In any case, the authority of a pope is not given to him by those who choose him, even though the *method* of choosing was indeed bindingly determined by the deceased pope, or an earlier one before him, so long as a pope may not designate whom his successor should and will be. (Heaven forbid! There are those "papalists" who cannot conceive of a boundless-enough authority of the popes, who seem to think that such an "election" would not be impossible because some future pope might believe the method to be opportune, and therefore, in principle, they think it to be legitimate. Such extreme papalists might well consider the example of Felix III, who in 530 chose his successor, Boniface II, in this manner.) This is a fundamental juridical action in the church that occurs without a pope. Now, however, the realistic pragmatists in the church will say, It cannot be otherwise; it has always been this way, what is there to get excited about? When there is a new pope, then he is pope and has the right to affirm [his election]. Period. But "one is still entitled to ask the question." at least according to Hans Habe.[g] Why should this right be refused to theologians in the church?

And so let us prescind for now from the argument that the designation of later popes by those who came before would make our question unproblematic, even though one could suggest that such a "mode of election" would be more in keeping with the spirit of Vatican I than the current method, for then the full, supreme and universal jurisdictional authority of the pope would be yet more clearly present. We will also prescind from the argument that one might ask how long a papal election might be put off, or how long it might continue, even for quite sensible reasons. We will prescind because, to my knowledge, there is not a single positive juridical determination about this question (the schedule for the *beginning* of the conclave is quite different). Other constitutions set time limits for similar cases, and such might be sensible here also, especially when one thinks of the longer conclaves. We will not ask here *why*, in fact, a pope does not designate his successor, and as this does not appear impossible in light of Vatican I, grounds could certainly be conceived in which such a process might seem warranted. In any case, however, here is an authority—relevant to the entire church and of fundamental importance—for making legal decisions that is not the pope, and to whom the pope does not belong, and to which he cannot belong as pope.

Now, how might one know that this can be true *only* in this one case, such that there are no other cases in which such a case might be more generally true? Would it not, for example, be possible (or even *should* it be) for an institutional board in the church to be established regarding the contemporary secular and ecclesial situation with which the pope must grapple today, which could provide the possibility of a "brotherly" admonition to the pope regarding his administration of his office? Such a committee, to which the pope might not belong, might even have the responsibility in certain situations for reaching a binding conclusion (itself a juridical procedure) without his direct authority or input. Such a body could certainly be reconciled with the prerogatives of the papal office and still have binding authority in the church. Must any such division of powers at the highest levels of the church be simply contrary to the teaching of the First Vatican Council? Could it not be opportune, even if one naturally must allow from the first (as it is within nations) that the officeholders who wield some of the pope's own discharged authority (however one thinks of this, and which in most cases can be understood as being discharged in unity with the papal prerogative) would finally be appointed by the pope? Couldn't such a division of power not be exactly as possible in the church (*de iure humano*) as when the pope has agreed through concordats with the secular powers to some binding agreement regarding the naming of bishops? Might not decisions be possible within a particular church that the pope simply and certainly *must* leave to the particular church alone (for natural-law or other reasons), otherwise, explicitly or implicitly, any autonomy of the particular churches would seem to be abrogated by the authority of the pope? How then do things stand in the *summation* of the particular churches, which themselves legally reach these decisions apart from the pope (i.e., at least without a positive legal action on his part)?

And even if the decision during a papal election were to be the single act "apart from the pope," it still remains true that in the church, there is a bearer of a most important authority, who is not identical with the pope either entirely or in part. The bearer of this authority also has their power from God, or from the church, to the extent that the church is a reality of the highest spiritual variety desired by God and that it is capable of providing itself a pope, and as this exists, it must therefore be possible. At this point it becomes clear that the pope and his authority—at least concerning the character of a particular pope, and therefore also concerning the particular character of his authority—is dependent on a reality that is not identical with him but predates him. If one wishes to discount this and answer, "This reality is the will of God or [for those wishing to invoke Christ himself] Christ's will as founder of the church," then one must still ask how and wherein this will of God or of Christ is made present concretely in the world to us. One might then answer, "In the community of believers itself in the church, never abandoned by the Spirit of God, who always—including through every *sede vacante*—always constitutes anew its full social tangibility and public character, but always already as such that it is capable as a legal entity, even *prior to* each act, and so gives itself over to its pope, who then has every prerogative that (as already stated by Vatican I) belongs necessarily to the church."

One must, therefore, say that the church as a whole is the proper and original bearer of all powers that are present in her in her various officeholders. She, in her entire reality of spirit and belief, provides the space such that something like the authority of her officeholders might be possible in the first place. This does not mean that these various kinds of authority could be kept to herself and regularly exercised without the existence of concrete officeholders. The church's being is structured so that concrete administration of her authority requires that she appoint such actual officeholders, for it is demanded by the substance of the matter itself, even if it is otherwise in at least one case—that is, in the appointment of the highest bearer of her authority himself. Even this appointment must be undertaken by concrete people, although one cannot say *de iure divino* whom these should be. But, therefore, one must think of the church in such a way that we can understand how this is possible for her. This, however, means that there is a legal entity, "the church," that can take action, at least in those cases in which an institutionalized officeholder *iuris divini* is not conceivable or, we might add, is not possible.

As one last example, without grasping after excuses, and without merely accepting what has been assumed so far, how could one account for the Council of Constance's overcoming of the great schism? Was the validity of the election of Martin V after the resignation of his predecessors dependent on the strictly voluntary character of these resignations, or is the fact that their successor was universally acknowledged enough? If the second case, however, which qualities of an officeholder must the church recognize in advance as belonging to any particular bearer of papal authority? During the *de auxiliis* controversy, the Spanish Jesuits discussed the question, much to the annoyance of the then-current pope, of whether it belonged to the deposit of the faith to believe the current pope to be a legitimate pope. No matter how one answers this question, the conviction in the conscience of the normal Catholic of the legitimacy of any particular pope is grounded in the undisputed recognition of that pope by the Catholic Church. And when classical theology clarifies that a pope could become a heretic, and by this act itself cease to be pope, how else should the absence of such (public) heresy be established with sufficient certainty, except through the fact that the church does not recognize such heresy in her pope? Therefore, does not the legitimate character of a pope have conditions that are rooted in the church instead of in himself? Does this not remain true even if in the latter case one is not inclined to recognize in the act of ecclesial recognition of the pope an actual juridical act?

However dull-witted theologians and canonists are capable of being in this matter, one can make the case yet clearer to them via the following observation. Vermeersch[h] says, If a pope falls into notorious heresy, then he ceases, *ipso facto*, to be pope; for this, a *sententia declaratoria* relating to this notorious heresy is not necessary, because it is impossible. A pope may be judged by no one (according to Code of Canon Law [CIC] of 1917 can. 1556).[i] Now, naturally, such a heretic ceases, ipso facto, to be pope. But why then shouldn't it be possible to provide a *sententia declaratoria* about this? For the one against whom the judgment is made is no longer pope, and so can. 1556 does not apply to him. And anyway,[8] why shouldn't there be a medium for such a juridical declaration of this kind? Because at such a time as this, there would be no pope? Because such a responsibility is not assignable? But there is indeed a more juridically powerful act: the papal election itself. And so there *is* such a medium, no matter whether one understands the College of Cardinals to be capable of both acts (i.e., determining that the pope is a heretic and electing his successor) without a deeper grounding, or whether (based on a fuller ecclesiology), one reckons that this College of Cardinals represents the College of Bishops and the rights it possesses *iuris divini* (which must be well-differentiated from the rights of the College of Cardinals). For it is the Episcopal College that possesses by divine right the ability from God to affirm these two acts, even if the papal election itself must be (*de iure humano*) carried out by the College of Cardinals.

At this point, one might even ask if the church fundamentally, due to its very nature, must always grant its authority only to a single bearer or if there are situations in which a small group (a "synod") could be entrusted with this authority in all the particulars that the First Vatican Council ascribes to the pope. This question has not arisen because, since the beginning of the second century in the entire church, we have known only the monepiscopal structure

---

8. Literally, "above all."

of one bishop bearing authority over each particular church[9] and therefore have also had this constitution in Rome. Because of the existence of the Apostolic College and other very early presbyteral governance structures of particular churches,[10] one could consider the possibility that the leadership of particular churches could be imagined in the image of the Apostolic College, and therefore be synodally composed. One no longer traces back the authority of a particular bishop to a particular apostle. When, therefore, one traces back the authority of the Episcopal College to that of the Apostolic College, one grounds the authority of the particular bishop in the authority of the bishops as a college. Therefore, the question of whether a single particular church[11] might also be ruled on the model of the Apostolic College is not ridiculous a priori.

In any case, it is clear that two questions must be distinguished: the question about the content of a particular authoritative act and the question regarding the (individually or collectively understood) bearers of that authority. I do not accept [the argument] that the teaching of the church (e.g., in the Second Vatican Council) regarding the nature of the episcopal office is necessarily denied by accepting that episcopal authority might be borne by a small group. Is there a single historical heresy that is explicitly rejected that, while fully accepting the content and the provenance of the episcopal or papal authority, taught only that the *bearer* of such an authority could also be conceived of collegially? Such a heresy is not known to me. But is such a teaching, therefore, heretical? Is it enough to warrant this description that so far—that is, since the beginning of the second century—this bearer has always been conceived of in a monarchical fashion? Can one say with certainty that doubting or denying the necessity of the *monarchical* nature of the bearer of primacy or episcopacy is to be called heretical according to the

---

9. *Einzelnen Gemeinden.*
10. *Gemeindeverfassungen.*
11. *Bischofskirche.*

ordinary magisterium? Are there not many examples of teachings that were considered in light of some particular structure without any doubt for centuries and that are obligatory—whose sense can and must *now* be considered apart from this particular context (e.g., original sin with/out monogenesis)?

That the Second Vatican Council in its teaching about the episcopal office was thinking only and self-evidently of a *monarchical* bishop appears to me to not necessarily imply that a *presbyteral* organization of the episcopal office is incompatible with the nature of this office. The question, however, naturally arises then as to how one might conceive of such a collegial bearer of the episcopal office more explicitly, especially regarding juridical structure and function. This is entirely separate from the question of whether something like this is once again opportune, such that there could once again be such structures in the contemporary church. But at least the potential for them existed in the New Testament church. In no case can one say that the dogmatic and universal constitutional law of the church a priori and always denied the possibility of a collective wielder of authority. This constitutional law knew explicitly and without prejudice precisely such a collective agent—the Episcopal College. Granted, this is always with and under the pope. (By the way, "under" can only be used rather inexactly; for when one says "under," one thinks of the total number of single bishops with the exception of the pope, but this collection without the pope is not the Episcopal College.) But this is not an advisory board of the highest officials of the church gathered around the pope; it is itself the collective institution of the highest authority in the church, even if this institution itself has its own [internal] structure.

If, then, a collective authority-bearing agent exists (and is therefore possible) within the church, even according to Catholic ecclesial constitutional law, how might one definitively and certainly prove that according to this constitutional law, *iuris divini*, such a thing *can only* exist in the case in which it actually exists today, such that, for example, a presbyteral council could not lead a particular church in principle, or that the bearer of supreme Petrine authority *can only* be an individual? If we had other such collegial bearers of ecclesial authority, then difficulties would arise regarding how such a body ought be structured to make it capable of acting. But this difficulty would not be greater than that which exists in any case (and has yet to be solved with convincing clarity): that is to say, the College of Bishops itself and its relationship to the pope. Should someone wish to reject this suggestion, he would even then require one who would wield authority on his own, even in the case of a Presbyterial College. One is then back in the situation of the Episcopal College, for one would once again have a bishop of the contemporary kind at the helm—that is, one who could act within such a college, as in our case, *primus inter pares*. Second, If this college had a leader, like a contemporary bishop, who also held the power of the college alone, such a thing demonstrates itself to be plausible. For it is clearly not impossible according to Catholic dogmatic teaching about the Episcopal College, even if so far no one has yet demonstrated it exactly, to imagine a (even if partial) *double* summit in the church, unless one insists that the pope—even when he acts alone—is still operating as the representative of the entire college. But then another question arises regarding in what sense the pope must operate when he is making his own decisions, such that one can sensibly say that he operates always as the representative of the episcopal college. This is especially so because it would seem he could do this only when he received the consent of the college to his actions in a juridically defined manner. The answers to these questions are still obscure.

3. The Nature of the Church Unfolding in History[12]

If one wishes to univocally assert and prove absolutely for certain that episcopacy and primacy can only be conceived of *monarchically*, several assumptions, themselves problematic, would have to be made. One might assume that the structure of the church at the end of the apostolic era with *all* its particularities is *iuris divini* and therefore unchangeable. But how would one prove this? Could one honestly imagine a nonmythological scenario by which the concrete manner of the means of the revelation and founding of the church could be understood such that it was truly explicitly revealed that all of these particularities, whose existence can be explained simply by the cultural and social conditions of the historical church, are necessary to fulfill the foundational desires of Jesus for the church? Or that an apostle had explained this to be so? (Assuming, of course, that such an apostle be understood in a formal manner as being equivalent to Jesus as a primary bearer of revelation, which traditionally happens without our exactly saying so.) When someone wishes to explain the previous postulate by these means, he ends up with a mythological understanding of revelation that cannot be accepted today. In the other direction, one could just as well ask the question of from what part of revelation one knows that the Episcopal College has the authority that the Second Vatican Council recognizes it as possessing. Is Jesus's statement to the Twelve enough of a proof? Is the argument from the conciliar practice of the early

---

12. "Das Wesenrecht der Kirche und seine geschichtliche Verwirklichungen" could also be translated something like "The Ecclesial Essence Expressed in Law and Its Historical Emergence." In a 1974 talk collected in *TI*, vol. 17, called "Transformations in the Church and Secular Society," Rahner remarks that he has suggested a "'law based on the nature of the Church,' as the foundation for its hierarchical structure" (168n2). As this lecture was not published originally in German, the translation in the *TI* is the only source I have for this remark, but as Rahner points to the *Vorfragen* in the note, I have taken this as the title of this section.

church compelling? How can one think of the original revelation of this teaching such that it can also be considered a historical development? Can one arrive at this idea without accepting that the church (which in its earliest sense as a legal subject, or a being, is the congregation of believers gathered around the Risen One as the invincibly victorious eschatological event) has understood itself to be an actor within a historical process such that its very self-understanding (which is revelation) comes into being within this history, and accept that both it and its self-consciousness also exist from the earliest beginnings of the church? With this, we come to a second possibility that must be considered.

In order to answer our problem, one could begin from the assumption that there exists in the church a development that *could have* developed differently (insofar as one can picture such alternate histories from the historical record), which, however, is actually rendered *irreversible* in the course of history such that this outcome can be understood to be *iuris divini*, despite the possibility that it might not have been so in apostolic times, or even in the times during which the canonical Scriptures were arising. I have developed a theory of just such a *ius divinum* over some years.[j] I believe, in regard to the question of the constitution of the church, that such a theory is required in order to explain, among other things, how we can count something as belonging to the church's constitution *de iure divino*, even though there is little or no evidence that it existed at the time of the apostles or of the New Testament as the only option, or that it was then understood to be an unchangeable aspect of the church's makeup. But there are two things that must quickly be said about such a theory and its role in the current investigation:

First, in considering the theory that I have laid out here, one does not immediately see why objects of the divine law must only be grounded in the apostolic era, although most theologians (for some reason) firmly believe that for a thing to be *de iure divino*, it must be revealed and therefore must be at least implicitly present in the apostolic age and visible by the end of that era. Why shouldn't a historical entity also be able to make binding decisions in its later life in light of its self-knowledge of its essence and development, and not only at its beginning? These decisions develop out of the actual historical character of the church into a situation such that only one choice remains possible. Why can't this also be possible for the church? Why can't one consider some later judgments of the church about its nature to be *ius divinum*, as they are both essential and irreversible? Even if this cannot apply to all the church's decisions, it could apply to some and may actually apply to a few.

The second thing that must be demonstrated, and not assumed, is that the *monarchical* character of those bearing episcopal or papal offices is revealed as *ius divinum* in the church. Therefore, according to the present theory, it is at best an implementation of this *ius divinum*. But is this conviction really explicitly mandated, or does one say it only because one, in describing the offices concerned, is doing so within a dogmatic duty that is itself defined by those holding the offices being described? Because one is used to describing it in this way and a change would not be opportune? Isn't it similar to the fact that the highest leader in the church defines himself as the *Roman* bishop, although it is not dogmatically certain that the bearer of the highest office in the church must be for all time the Bishop of Rome? Therefore, the question can remain open whether, and under what unforeseeable conditions, a change in this matter might legitimately be made.

There is much that remains clouded in the dogmatic teaching about the constitution of the church, especially if one does not accept everything that is as immediately self-evident or assume that one can distinguish between *ius divinum* and *ius humanum* in the actual constitution of the church without first undertaking to explicitly reflect on criteria. It is also difficult if the tacit conviction is that practically everything in the contemporary church that an unreflective examination might consider to be permanent is, for that reason alone, the final faith conviction of the church or a dogma deriving from the ordinary magisterium. So one cannot think that because one knows that on the one hand the concrete form of the church developed in history and therefore made use of much that came from its historical situation and on the other that the earliest revelation of Christianity is of Jesus as the crucified and risen one and therefore as the absolute savior, that nothing else is binding. What else could the earliest Christian revelation have been? When we say that Jesus founded the church and instituted the sacraments, these ideas must be understood (unless they lose their historical plausibility) to mean that the church and the sacraments are grounded in that which Jesus experienced in faith, what he himself was and wanted to be, and so they are desired by him. One cannot, naturally, deny that historically in the life of Jesus, various things (such as the Eucharist, the Apostolic College, Jesus's own baptism, etc.) are concretely present and anticipate the future that would unfold and so verify these as legitimate developments. But these coherences initially have only a historical weight. Historically, what Jesus himself possibly arranged can only be recognized as forever valid and compulsory because and insofar as these realities and connections are borne by an original and enduring connection between Jesus as the ultimate savior and the community of faith (i.e., the church) that confesses Jesus as the savior and that in historically traceable and legitimate ways descends from him and is therefore *dogmatically* legitimized.

It would appear to be noteworthy that the scholastic tradition of the church recognizes a "natural law" that precedes the positive law, no matter how one understands more exactly the analogous being of this natural law to positive law, or the relationship between the two. In any case, there is such a law, it is given by God to us along with our human nature, it can be applied, and so on. Why shouldn't we also recognize, analogous to this law, a law flowing from the nature of the church and given with that nature? This simple, essential law[13] of the church cannot be simply identified with the *ius divinum* of the church. Then it would indeed be conceived of as a kind of positive law—that is, as explicitly stated norms deriving from the externally expressed will of God (and Christ) for the church that are manifested as clear propositions. The positive (secular) law and the typical understanding of the *ius divinum* of the church exist as propositions in their primary reality; only the legislator of these propositions differs. The essential law that I intend here can also be objectivized into propositions, even fundamentally. The question, however, can remain open as to how far the *ius divinum* is to be thought of as the complete working out of this essential law of the church, and to what extent it might be understood merely as the working out of a variety of attendant, but extrinsic, factors. But in any case, there is an essential law of this kind, because even before the propositions of the *ius divinum* (at least as typically understood), there was a church in reality: a final union of world, humanity, and history; a self-revelation of God in his Spirit in the world, through which he makes himself to be the most inner principle,[14] potential, and unreachable goal of that world. The Crucified and Risen, in whom this eschatologically victorious self-revelation of God appears and is made irreversible in history; and that which is important and ultimate in this Crucified, Risen One is given to community of faith that is gathered in his Spirit, which bears witness to his victory and always makes him present in history, and so on. Through it, a real "being" exists from which an essential law flows. Much that is in the explicit, propositional law of the church, the *ius divinum*, may belong to this essential law, and *therefore* has been explicitly formulated. But it cannot be assumed that this

---

13. Here, he speaks of a *Wesenrecht*, a right flowing from the essence of the church, not *Naturrecht*, the usual language for natural law as applied above, although clearly the ideas are related.

14. *Entelechy.*

essential law is exhausted or adequately expressed by this proposi-tional law, as is testified to by both scholastic ecclesiology and the explicit teaching of the magisterium on the church. Here, in our context, the point is not to articulate individual canons[15] and their relationship to the essential law. But one must see that such essential laws hold within them the possibilities in particular circumstances of bringing forth authorized legal norms (e.g., on the sacraments) when necessary and when given with authority in light of the cir-cumstances, when the extant norms are not sufficient. One should not, however, jump the gun in such situations. When the usual norm is insufficient, one shouldn't immediately appeal to God, his grace, and his sovereignty so as to claim that it is a matter bound up in the law given by him for us. We shouldn't be too quick to leave the realm of the historical, societal, ritual, and so on.

Strangely enough, theologians have speculated about a "natural sacrament" existing during pre-Christian times in order that chil-dren might have been reached by the incarnation of God's sav-ing will through social and historical realities. In the new covenant, however, so that God's grace would be even greater and more incarnate, one leaves children who die unbaptized to drift about in limbo. One allows the saving will of God, even understood as "general" and "infralapsarian," to founder on his own law of bap-tism. If normal baptism cannot be given, one does not allow grace to function beyond the sacrament. And (this is important for us) one doesn't even trouble himself to ponder a remedy analogous to the "natural sacrament" proceeding from the nature of the church. Why shouldn't something like this exist? Is the new covenant poorer than the old? Will fewer people be saved in it than in the old in an at least quasi-sacramental manner?

May not a contemporary theologian postulate such a natural sacrament, just as Augustine, Thomas,[k] and others did, even though they also couldn't reference an explicit revelation? Might one not

---

15. Or "propositions"—*Rechtssätze*.

consider the spirit of accepting a person into the community of persons as such a natural sacrament, if and insofar as it receives this meaning as a sign of healing arising from the being of the church (as the primordial sacrament of mercy in the world) and leads back to the church as a sign of the mercy of God in the world in the particular situation in which each person exists? When the theologians of the past say that the natural sacrament did not function *ex opere operato*, this means nevertheless that it did function (however this efficacy is to be conceived). Such a "natural sacrament" might indeed function *ex opere operato* in the scope of the eschatologically victorious church, even if it did not earlier, precisely because the normal sacraments function in this way.

If one were to read the considerations so far quickly and in a superficial manner, one would doubtless get the impression that they are completely mixed up and unsystematic. If, however, one attends more sympathetically and precisely, one will indeed soon find the connection to our original question, the mutual recognition of ministries between the churches. As has been said before, in this work, I am only proposing a preliminary consideration of the topic, no more. There are no proper theses on the basic question. However, at this point, at least so far as I hope, the scope of the questions is becoming clear. Cannot one consider the church as a juridic person, both when the complete hierarchal structure of the church in the Catholic sense lay in the future and also once it had legitimately constructed itself into this concrete constitution and so was bound to all of the details? Is it not possible to imagine that other legislation might tacitly emanate from this more primordial being—which would also be the responsibility of the papacy, at least in certain cases, due to God's desire for the salvation of all people in all their conditions and situations—without thereby denying the concreteness of the church's actual essence, into which this being has developed in essence in space and time?

As a second basic question, might it not be the case that the church gives authorization for particular sacramental acts deriving from its original nature to particular recipients, even if these minis-tries are not constituted in the exact same way that is legitimate and therefore binding for all those within the Catholic Church (monar-chical, etc.)? And yet might these ministers nevertheless be bearers of such an authorization within particular conditions and under specific historical situations? Are the ways in which the argument about ministry is most often constructed and the assumptions from which this argument proceeds really the only possibilities? Or are there other starting points on different levels that both are deeper and yet might have juridical effects? Yet again, these are no longer questions. For hopefully it need no longer be emphasized that con-sidering the possible flexibility of the structure of offices in the Catholic Church is of significance for the "question of ministries" that is the theme of this work. If such a flexibility *is* compatible with the nature of the church according to Catholic understand-ing, then one may *not* begin the "question of ministries" with the implicit assumption that only those ministries in other churches that exactly mirror the contemporary expression of order in the Catholic Church can ever possibly be considered legitimate.

3
Recognizing Reality

One can demonstrate both the contingency and the accidental nature of the explicit juridical structures and acts of the church in terms of their original being, which in itself is a source of law, as well as through a number of other considerations. How does, for example, a priest know that he is validly ordained? If he predicates this validity only on an unbroken chain of valid ordinations (validity being understood in the usual way) beginning with the bishop who ordained him and stretching back to the apostles, considering the conditions of validity according to the usual measures (including also internal intention, perhaps in the Middle Ages the very particular *traditio instrumentorum*, and the many other terms that apply or have applied), then this priest must say that (morally) he, at the very best, can presume a likelihood for the validity of his ordination. He must trust to the benevolent providence of God that there have not been too many invalid ordinations in this extensive ordination chain, since the conditions set for a valid ordination can be easily disrupted without anyone noticing. Is such a notion sensible? Is the nature of the thing it describes suitable and worthy of God? I don't think so. The entire idea presupposes a "physical" conception of the conditions of validity, a presupposition that does not accord with the nature of the thing it supposes to describe.

What really can stand against this conception can be conceived thus: the priest or bishop is validly ordained if he as is recognized as such by the church without dissent. This fact of the open acceptance of a bishop or priest by his church constitutes the validity of his ordination. What one usually sees as requirements and prerequisites of a valid ordination are in truth the fulfillment of the "normal" rules, according to which the (hierarchically structured) public church pronounces its judgment of validity. These rules, however, because they were made by the church in its concreteness, are rules that it gives itself along with the duty to follow them. As their degree and extent is dependent on its own will, and so they are not themselves an authority over against the church and its judgment. These norms, therefore, remain unaffected and undamaged if the church itself wishes to deviate from its customary procedure: for example, by recognizing an ordination as valid, in spite of such norms. Of course, one can posit against this argument that the church acts, at least in analogous cases, on the contrary assumption.

So for example, a *putative marriage*[1] is considered invalid, when even thirty years after marriage, a formal defect is discovered in the rite although the marriage had been regarded as valid by the spouses and the public church and lived as such for thirty years. But is this typical interpretation of such a wedding as invalid correct? Or is it false? Why should one not simply call this interpretation false, if only because doing so is nonsensical to a normal human sensibility and, as a matter of fact, the marriage might be found to be real, even if it was originally contracted wrongly or in violation of the normal rules of validity? That cases exist in which such an opinion is difficult to support is not itself a counterargument. An absolute, always-present connection between the moral and human on the one hand and the real or putatively just on the other does

---

1. See CIC 1917 can. 1015 §4 and 1983 can. 1061 §3: "An invalid marriage is called putative if at least one party celebrated it in good faith, until both parties become certain of its nullity."

not exist in the life of the church in any case. Thus, according to the customary practice of today's church, upon discovering a formal deficit prior to the *sanatio in radice*, if the church permitted another marriage to a different spouse, then the church is merely wrong. Similar mistakes might also be found in the case in which, after the judgment of nullity by an ecclesiastical court, later found to be objectively wrong, a new marriage has been contracted, or in the cases where the popes of the Middle Ages gave permission for a divorce, which, according to current opinion, is impossible. Returning to the thirty-year marriage we are considering, it can be recognized as valid because of its long public recognition. The renewed marriage or *sanatio in radice* can be understood as an explicit maintenance of this already-present validity in the aftermath of the earlier formal error.

From this perspective, it becomes both understandable and unobjectionable to assert that one cannot be certain that centuries of ordinations were completed according to ritual and fulfilled the requirements for validity—whatever the required ritual was (the laying on of hands, or the *traditio instrumentorum*, or both, or anther ritual pertaining to ordination). Under whichever undeliberated-upon rite one had publicly conferred and maintained the status of a legitimate and recognized priest in the church, he *had* precisely this status, and therefore it was clear. If, however, one presumes an understanding of ministry that is almost physicalist and depends on very particular conditions—such that without this or that condition being fulfilled, an ordination, even if it remains unchallenged in the church, is invalid—suddenly the sacramental life of the church is in a dangerous situation. For in this situation, a legal uncertainty threatens [the church's life] and one must postulate a not-entirely believable divine providence that prevents the breaking of sacramental succession chains.

Perhaps, at this point, it would be sensible to provide a more explicit engagement with how we must think about the so-called *sanatio in radice* if we wish to understand it as a sensible legal event.

A marriage should have all the personal conditions and peculiarities necessary for a valid marriage but, if it lacks these, it will be considered "invalid" because of the formal error in the ritual. Now, the lawgiver dispenses from this lack of form,[2] and even does this in such a way that the the those married may not know of the dispensation, and yet the marriage is valid. According to the canonical presuppositions of this *sanatio in radice*, the spouses before this *sanatio* could have separated with a clean conscience and entered into another marriage, but now suddenly their marriage is indissoluble without the spouses knowing anything about this fundamental change in their existential state. Is this really reasonable? Can one find one's way through this plight merely by saying that in such a case, the spouses already had a "moral" duty to remain together (according to nature) and to aspire to a *sanatio in radice*? I say no. For even if they had not complied with this moral duty, according to the typical scholastic theology, any future marriage with another person could have nevertheless been considered valid.

But such a position seems to obviously contradict the moral norms of the gospel, which protect the moral with legal effects. So can one think of the *sanatio in radice* in such a way that we must not reject as senseless nor, as is more common, consider it to require explanation in order to appear sensible? It would seem that the case is simple: the earlier deficit in form had made the marriage (existentially and also socially) not actually invalid; the *sanatio in radice* merely recognizes explicitly that the lack of form that appeared to make the marriage impossible had not done so in this case. The lawgiver does not change the thing itself but redefines his own relationship to it. But from this we can see that a single social status in the church can arise—or at least can be recognized as having arisen—from

---

2. That is, the ecclesiastical authority has given a canonical dispensation (legal permission) for the circumstances that do not meet the legal requirements pertaining to form for a valid marriage.

differing means. A higher principle can override the usual narrower norms for what is sufficient or forbidden, and these may make something legal that has transgressed the usual norms. Of course (speaking generally) the case is conceivable that a given human reality (e.g., the conjugal-personal relationship of two people, a de facto function in a society) can—despite there existing the impediment of a lower norm, even before its explicit recognition—bear the name (the designation) by which this reality is recognized. And thus, this recognition appears as recognition of the *ex tunc* (i.e., as acknowledgment of the already-given reality as ever present). The case is also conceivable that the name (the designation), whatever for good or bad reasons, is only applied to the explicitly recognized reality, and therefore, in this sense, the reality is recognized to exist *ex nunc* (i.e., from the moment of that recognition). It can, of course, also be the case that such a reality evolves through *three* phases: an initially illegitimate constitution of such a reality, the later becoming-legitimate of that reality, and an explicit recognition of this reality as having become legitimate after its inception. One might consider, for example, a second marriage contracted during the life of the first spouse, the legitimizing of this second marriage following the death of the first spouse, and the explicit ecclesial recognition of the marriage. Or the illegitimate seizure of church property by the state, the legitimizing of the state's holding the property through the later development of a new historical and cultural situation and a long history of ownership, and the eventual recognition of this legitimacy by the church. Similarly, one might consider a bishop who, through his own decision, had become a schismatic. The church might not recognize some of the jurisdictional acts by which he entered into schism or that necessitated the church's protest. But a time might come in which the acts of a successor to this bishop are completely legitimate. Finally, a time might come in which also the Roman Catholic Church explicitly recognized his legitimacy. If we consider the example of how the church has engaged with the jurisdiction of schismatic bishops to hear confessions, we can see such a development in three phases as having actually existed in history.

One can, and must, differentiate within such an explicit kind of recognition between the *official* and *private*. One such example of the difference can be shown in history. Consider a marital bond between two Catholic Christians, one of whom had previously lived in a "marriage" that had certainly been invalid according to all the norms of morality and church law but, for which the invalidity, for whatever reason, could not be proven and recognized as such *in foro Ecclesiae*. Is this "second" marriage valid if it is registered in the civil office (analogous to CIC can. 1098)?[a] If yes, then at least those Christians who are aware of the details might recognize the marriage as a Christian, sacramental one, although it wouldn't and couldn't be recognized as such officially by the church. (The difference between the "details" and their public-juridical status in a community cannot be overcome in every case, even in the church.) Could a cleric who is convinced of the invalidity of the first "marriage" assist at the celebration of the "second" (assuming that it causes no scandal)? If yes, he is recognizing the second marriage as sacramentally valid, although no declaration of nullity relating to the first had been issued by the institutional church. Is such a thing only possible for marriage, or also might it happen with other sacraments? Can we also differentiate between a similar official and private recognition of such a sacrament?

What these questions might mean for the consideration of our main theme ought, at this point, to be clarified.

4

Sharing Salvation

1. Good and Bad Faith in a Time of Schism

In light of the basic question that has already been addressed, an entirely new consideration arises. It has to do with the relationship of the non-Catholic churches and ecclesial communities to the Roman Catholic Church according to the Catholic Church's own view. (And so we will not ask here how these other churches understand themselves or how they interpret their relationships to the Catholic Church.) Throughout this investigation, the (official and scholastic) Catholic teaching regarding this relationship is presumed to be valid.

Within these presuppositions, then, I am only seeking to further explore this "classical" teaching and make the implications that already exist within it clearer. One must, so it appears to me, first carefully ponder the fact that one ought to differentiate between the relationship of the Catholic Church to the other churches in the moment of the *origination* (according to the Catholic view) of heretical or schismatic churches, and the relationship that exists in a later age when these churches are no longer to be primarily understood in terms of their denial of the Catholic Church and/or its teachings. This distinction, however, was not clearly seen—even in recent history. This demonstrates, for example, that until very recently, the Catholic Church's apologetics understood bona fides to exist among the most uneducated, but not the theologically educated people among such heretics or schismatics. After the Second Vatican Council, no one can claim this any longer. However, one can certainly suggest that in the *emergence* of such a church-producing heresy or schism, people mutually imputed mala fides or assumed their existence to be self-evident. [Whether this was justified or not, what kind of procedure would have been required on both sides after the emergence of heresy and schism had both sides mutually presumed bona fides on both sides, and the question of whether Christians actually should have done what they did is not up for discussion.] The parties had this presumption of mala fides, as the evidence of the style of discussion in the emergence of ecclesial divisions and other evidence proves—even including direct expressions of this presumption. But this mutual assessment in light of the emergence of the split is taken for granted for later times, as are the practical consequences of the action that naturally derived from this presumption (leading to even those paintings in which Luther was represented as being the tool of the devil). This is despite the fact that the churches were no longer living, or rather living only, out of the *pathos* of the era of division, but instead were responding to the weight of their actual (separate) existences across many centuries. This separate existence led to their separation coming to seem expected. In the past, this historical development has not been attended to clearly enough. One considered the (completely uninvolved) children just as one had looked at their ancestors, to whom could not impute innocence and impartiality.

Now things are different. People communicate quite hopefully and lovingly with one another. The pope—for example—receives the leaders of the divided churches. Paul VI spoke unselfconsciously of "sister churches" whenever he spoke of the Orthodox churches. (It is not easy to see how such words can be squared up with the declaration in the first part of the Congregation for the Doctrine of the Faith's document of June 24, 1973, "Mysterium ecclesiae"

about the unique status of the Roman Catholic Church.[a] But that
is a question for a different paper.) This all seems self-evident. But
it is apparently not so clear. Leo X certainly did not approach Wit-
tenberg in the same way that Paul VI went to Geneva. Such an
action on the part of a pope during the Reformation era would
have seemed to be a betrayal of his own self-understanding. Today,
such actions are expected[1] among Christians because each feels
themselves to be the recipient of the fact of the separation, which
presents itself as a task for the future but does not necessarily judge
itself to have arisen from a desire to become separated in the past
despite everything we *know* about this past. And so, it is apparent
that people find no difficulty in recognizing between themselves a
genuine bona fides.

When the relevant decrees of Vatican II were completed, so
far as I know, no one agonized about *how* one could say all the
things that were said about the separated brethren, given that what
Vatican I said was also true: namely, that the divine origin of the
Roman Catholic Church is the most intelligible thing in the world,
accessible to every intelligence in every age. Thus, the conviction
now expressed or assumed of the (generally presumed) bona fides
of the others might not be so obvious. These implications of the
difference between the relationship of the separate churches—on
the one hand, in the situation of heresy or schism's first emergence,
and on the other hand, in the later situation—must suffice here,
however incomplete it may be.

However, this first historical and psychological distinction has
a theological-ecclesiological relevance on which we usually reflect
too little. The division of the churches (and therefore the necessity of a reunion) should not be denied or played down. But it is
more accurate to ask what kind of being, theologically speaking,

---

1. Here, Rahner is making an extended play on *Selbstverständlich* with all the
"clearly," "self-evident," and related terms being played against the pope's own
"self-understanding."

this separateness has if one must recognize the bona fides of the separated churches and they mutually recognize it in one another. In this question, it should be noted that this recognition of bona fides is to be regarded as a historical, public fact, determined as such by proven data, and not merely as a private matter involving individuals. These communally held bona fides of the other churches—which, of course, do not say anything about the individuals in such churches—can be understood analogically to the church's "holiness" as a public and historically tangible entity, even though about the holiness of the individual, nothing is certain. These bona fides, when mutual, are recognized such that on each side, they constitute a reality that on the other's side can be acknowledged, and this creates a unity of an ecclesiological nature, whatever the separation is. This unity is neither simply identical to the (rightly emphasized today) already-given unity of separated Christians in Christ and his mercy, nor identical to the (also rightly emphasized) commonality of the many Christian possessions (such as baptism, the Bible, etc.) that exist in the separated churches (but which are better seen as a commonality that exists separately in the different churches). Of course, all of these belong to a (single) unity as constituent moments, for they are interrelated and contribute to the ability to recognize in one another bona fides. For, if people mutually experience these fruits, they may recognize the Gifts of the Spirit in the other. Theologically, however, one has not yet clearly seen the already-given unity of separated churches if one does not consider these public and mutually recognized bona fides. If, however, one does see these bona fides in this way—such that in the separate churches, they universally allow for, or are factually identical with, the salvific faith—then it is implicitly understood that the separated churches (as a whole, without making judgments about the individual as such) are not, in reality, separated such that in the ultimate depths of [God's] saving being, salvation would be impossible. The churches are separated, but it is recognized that they are not separated today by an act occurring here and now.

Total separation can only be achieved by such an act that abolishes the salvific faith and—in this way—the bona fides.

Now one can further ask, In the dimension of public, official, and compulsory confessions, are there (still today) such theological differences existing on both sides by a genuine (at least attempted) faith commitment, such that there is a real separation through heresy and not only through schism? Or is it the case that in the Orthodox and Protestant churches, there exists no officially[2] prescribed teaching that exerts a single and direct positive duty for a faith commitment that would lead to the denial of a defined Catholic teaching? (At least insofar as teaching on the papacy is concerned, its never having come to pass among the Orthodox churches did not prevent the qualification of these as merely schismatic by Catholics, because the rejection of this doctrine is not a dogmatically absolutely required datum on the part of Eastern Orthodoxy. Its nonacceptance on the Protestant side is similarly not grounded by an absolute no. Meanwhile, on the Catholic side, it is not certain that a positive acceptance in terms of *faith* of the kind made by the First Vatican Council must always and in every case be demanded of every member of the Catholic Church.) But even here, might some number of things be excluded from the category of "obligatory doctrine" that are usually understood to be such in the Catholic sense of the faith when one sees this faith-consciousness from the viewpoint of the sense of faith that has been [officially] unfolded by the office[holders] of the church? But if that is so, then the peculiarity of this not-totally-divided division becomes even clearer: the divided churches are not separated from one another by an absolutely binding "no." They have unity in the Spirit and in many inherited Christian commonalities; they recognize one another with a publicly demonstrable bona fides, which implies a truly salvific Christian faith. Whatever the historical origin of separation may have been, the split coexists with the mandate and the duty

---

2. *Amtlich*—so also required by the office/ministry holder.

of consensus and, in that sense, is from the standpoint of faith and theology a nonessential. Indeed, the separation today is often in itself merely a social and historical fact, the nature and weight of which is different than (we must presume) was the case in the *act* of separation (and, importantly, this action happened on *both* sides!). Similarly, the act of provoking an improper state and the state that persists thereafter are or may be considered two completely different things both humanly and morally.

When the *nota explicativa praevia* to *Lumen gentium* states in no. 2 that the present and legitimate exercise of *munera* (offices or ministries) in the church would require a canonical mandate beyond consecration, even if in the life of the church, according to the circumstances of the time, these can already exist prior to their codification in law.[b] Then it must also be said that when and where such a *legal* authorization process is required for the exercise of an office, one must adhere fundamentally to this legal standardization, in order for the act of such an official to be legitimate. But the possibility of their being made legitimate by the uncodified *life* of the church is not simply abolished in cases where such codification does not occur. Given how difficult it is to bring morality and law to coincidence in every case, one cannot insist from the outset that the legally codified process of a sacramental action is, even after such a codification, the only conceivable case in which the sacramental event of grace can come into being or that only *before* such a codification could the church's "life" (the expression of the *Nota praevia!*[c]) be capable of constituting a grace-conveying act as sacramental. Life is not bound from the outside by acts of codification, although it binds *itself* to the codified manner of its implementation, but only to the extent that it does not contradict itself. Wherever a contradiction against code is also a contradiction of the church's life itself (such as in a culpable public disobedience to the law, in case of avoidable "disorder," etc.), even the "life" of such a perpetrator denies this necessary legitimacy. But how else could it be? If the *Nota praevia* achieves some progress beyond the received doctrine of canon law toward a greater realism of historical thought and counteracts a historically unjustifiable exclusion of the present legal practice, as Ratzinger rightly says in his commentary on this *Nota*,[d] why should the intention only be to correct the understanding of the past and not also to provide a renewed grounding for the practice of the present, whose legitimacy within the framework of the normal will not be threatened by such a "relativization"? If one takes the normal practice of sacramental powers (etc.) too absolutely—that is, if one regards them from the outset as the only possible form at all—then one puts the meaning of the sacramental sign in danger: then all grace-related preexistent events outside of the normal sacramental realm would no longer have any internal relation to this sacramental realm and still be effective. The sacramental then appears to be a purely positive addition to the actual event of mercy, which occurs mostly apart from the sacramental (and so why not consider this situation normal?). If one wants to escape this danger and therefore emphasizes also for these cases a "subordination" to the historical-social, and therefore sacramental, domain of the church (as a non-Christian person *bonae voluntatis* is "ordered to" the church), then one can at least ask the question of whether this "ordering" is, at least in certain cases, such that it can and must be called sacramental, even though it does not fully correspond to the codified norms (that were established for good reasons). The domain of law also knows many cases in which valid legal relationships or subsets that do not conform to the generally accepted positive norm are nevertheless recognized as being valid under certain circumstances. If someone wanted to say that these are allowable because of more general norms (e.g., regarding an actor without a specific remit operating under general norms), then one would be required to ask whether such general norms might also be present in the sacramental field, even if they are not explicitly formulated.

One ought not say of all such considerations, "Let the church understand itself 'narrowly,' that does no harm! It cannot and does not want to narrow the work of God's grace itself; he remains sovereign regarding his mercy." So might one console oneself, if it should turn out for a Catholic theologian that the church wants to understand its action in a "narrow" way that is binding on it (and perhaps it thinks that because of revelation, it has to do that). But first of all, the Catholic theologian has the right and the duty to try to understand the church and its "radius of action" as broadly as possible. The realm of the salvific potential of God and his Christ and the realm of the church are not simply the same (no one would, for example, claim that an unbaptized person could encounter the Eucharist as a sacrament in the strongest sense of the word). Therefore, the realm of the church must not be restricted more than is absolutely necessary if it is to be the sign of God's universal salvific will for the whole world.

The next question that must be asked is this: Is not the ecclesiological milieu of these separate churches—always understood from a Catholic point of view—such that the acts that happen there and are conceived there are, if they are such that (at least *ex nunc*) they are recognized by the Catholic Church as granting the possibility of salvation, also valid and effective acts of a sacramental nature? Why shouldn't one be able to answer this question positively? Why wouldn't such a recognition be possible? And if in the last analysis, such acts are *recognized* as valid, and if they are valid *because* they are recognized—if they *can* be recognized because the normal rite of ordination is not necessary even in exceptional cases such that it is the only legitimate rite, and that ecclesial authority possibly exists in such a minister who belongs (within the separated churches) to a structure that is not in itself precluded by the nature of the church—can it not then be said that the bearers of such acts have an office? Or if one wants to reserve the word *office* only for those particularly commissioned—that is, where there is the possibility of grounding sacramental acts that the Catholic Church has received according to the "normal" manner (and not in the manner of a *sanatio in radice* but in the sense indicated above)—then avoiding the word *ministry*, one could still acknowledge the validity of these sacramental acts and validate them by acknowledgment (*quoad nos!*). Because on the one hand, they happen in an ecclesiological milieu in which such recognizable acts are possible. On the other hand— this brings us to the more radical question—by the presumption of the church (that is, according to the fundamental law arising from the church's being), they may be already recognized and therefore be truly valid.

One can still conceive of such acts as arising from the being of the church, even if they are already self-justified^e prior to any explicit recognition on the part of the ministers of the Catholic Church (of the kind of recognition received by the existing marriage that, although it began with a defect in form, received a *sanatio in radice*). Such a tacit recognition arising from the foundational nature of the church may well be accepted because such acknowledgment appears to be obligatory. One must therefore think the following: There are certainly bearers of powers who, while having a "moral" duty to use their authority for particular acts in certain situations, yet do not do so, and thus these acts do not exist. But one cannot easily apply this possibility in every case also to the church. As an eschatological presence of the salvation of God in the world, as the indestructibly "holy" church, particular acts must exist that the church not only *must not* but *cannot* refrain from completing. Why should not such acts also exist among those who act outside of the legal constitution [of the church], so that acts within the separated churches are also sacramentally legitimated and also might dare to expect an acknowledgment as such from the Catholic Church?

[As a side note: If a Protestant theologian should have the impression that in this way a substantial effort is being made to attempt to prove that their acts—which they themselves consider to be valid from the outset—are valid, and if they are upset that someone is seeking a Roman Catholic justification for them, then they must not overlook that the "whence" of this justification is the "foundational being" of the church, which is something the Catholic freely says "subsists" in their own concrete church (in order to speak with the Second Vatican Council[f]) according to its fully historical origins, but not as something that would not therefore be effective in their church. And finally, after all, ecumenically, the main thing would be that the sacraments and ministries in the Protestant churches could be seen to be recognizable by a Catholic from their own point of departure. To this point, something more will be said at the end.]

In the typical Catholic scholasticism, one often makes it too easy on oneself by wanting to grant such sacramental acts and "offices" a sort of *votum sacramenti* (desire for the sacrament) along with the gracious consequences sometimes accorded such a desire in Catholic scholasticism (and that it at least sometimes must grant) but that still permits denying the character of a sacrament or ministry as such. In doing so, it affirms this desire and the presence of the *res sacramenti* (at least in most cases) while denying that of the *sacramentum* [that is, the sign]. Such a ruling may be sufficient to satisfy an individual's anxiety about their salvation. But if one distinguishes too quickly between the sacramental signs and sacramental grace, there is danger that the sign will be devalued even to superfluity such that the graced reality that is signified can be received on its own without the sign (as in, for example, a union with Christ found through "spiritual communion" as a path to interpreting a Protestant Lord's Supper). But if the *sign* of grace also has meaning, if the entire order of salvation has an incarnate and sacramental character, why must we deny a sacramental character to the actions of the separated churches if, although their legitimacy cannot be recognized according to the (sensible and even necessary) normal laws of sacramental action, such a legitimacy can be rightly understood to arise from the foundational nature of the church itself?

2. Grace Outside of the Norm

Surely there is such a thing as an activity that commissions one to a new legal relationship in the church, a commission that is not explicit at all and that addresses a person who is not a member of the church in the straightforward and normal way. For this reason, for example, anyone, even a pagan, can validly baptize. Baptism, however, is a legal act that has the legal consequences of acceptance into the church. (Anyone who says that such a baptism has only to do with the establishment of a state of affairs and—while it certainly has legal consequences, that it need not itself be a juridical act—overlooks the fact that this "state of affairs" is a juridical act in itself and not only in its consequences, because it itself *is* the conferral of membership in the church. And this both factually and logically precedes the other effects of baptism.) How could such a baptism by a non-Christian be a legal act without presupposing a tacit commission given on the part of the church? One can certainly say that according to God's will, even a baptism by a heretic or a pagan is valid. But how do we know this? Cyprian had already argued that there was no revelation in the teaching of the apostles allowing this because, at the time of the apostles, there were no heretics performing baptisms.[g] And even if one doesn't find this and the other objections by Cyprian to be very convincing, one must still ask how this presumed validity of baptisms performed by heretics and pagans comes to be. (They are certainly not easy to refute; his opponents were only able to rely on their theologically unreflected-upon habitual practice; Augustine had to resort to postulating a "character for."[h] He had to attribute an effect to the baptism-by-heretic in order to be able to declare it to be good, though he would not recognize the gift of the Spirit itself in such a baptism, since this Spirit is only to be had within the *catholica*.) If one does not consider it reasonable to postulate an explicit revelation from the time of the apostles for the validity of baptism-by-heretic, which is certainly not obvious, and also has no more general principle it can point to and from which the later explanation the validity of the baptism-by-heretic can be deduced, then only the opinion, quite intelligible in itself, remains: The baptism-by-heretic is valid because it is considered valid by the church in a legally binding judgment such that the validity of this baptism therefore is not merely established by the church's later account but is itself rooted in this recognition. The question may well be left open whether the church could possibly have acted differently and therefore could have rejected baptisms-by-heretic as invalid or whether, for soteriological or moral reasons, it could not and therefore never did. Even if one wants to accept the latter option, and thus makes the nonreflective character of the decision historically easier to understand, this does not change anything in this creative legislative act by the church. For a legal act is a positive act even if the person who establishes that act is strictly morally obliged to enact it. Could one not say that the church should now reflect the sense, bearing, and proper internal motivation of what it did in the Donatism controversy of the third century regarding baptisms-by-heretic, and thus recognize that it can and must do likewise regarding the offices and sacramental authority of another kind? (In principle; the details and concrete preconditions of such an explicit recognition are not at issue here.) That is, in the separated churches (because the church, being holy and merciful, has always acted in this way out of its essential constitution, precisely because it must)?

One might now object that the subject of baptisms-by-heretic has nothing to say to more general questions, for by such a generalization, both too much and too little is demonstrated. *Too little* because it cannot be decided whether this process, which relates to the sacrament most necessary to salvation and is (in this context) relatively comprehensible, can be extended, for example, to include eucharistic authority. *Too much* because if indeed the pagan could validly baptize—that is, by the "construction" of an ecclesiological milieu, from which and on which basis the extraordinary and tacit authorization to ecclesiastical (sacramental) acts is conceivable—it is also too much, since the baptizing heathen does not belong to the milieu thus created. Or (viewed from the other perspective) because then one could ask why the pagan could not be authorized to preside at the eucharistic celebration, if from the validity of his baptizing one draws a conclusion about the possibility of a eucharistic celebration by those not "regularly" ordained.

But regarding the first objection (*too little*) one might next say that the validity of baptism-by-heretic at least demonstrates that such a tacit special commission for a sacramental-juridical act is not a priori impossible. If one were to say that because this is a sacrament that is absolutely necessary for salvation, and so here (but not elsewhere) everything must be possible, then it must be said that the teaching of the validity of a baptism-by-pagan is only an extension of the teaching of the validity of baptism-by-heretic. This teaching was not actually developed in view of *infant* baptism, and adult baptism does not demonstrate having such a pure necessity for salvation. If you push yet further, considering to what ecclesiological "distance" the commission of one pagan to receive another into the church extends (i.e., much further away from the church than in the cases that concern us) then one can say that in these cases the church "wagers" much less than in baptism-by-heretic, the validity of which does not even make the church dependent on the bona fides of the baptizer. Why shouldn't the church allow herself the right or the courage, in an analogous way, to do even less than she had already done in the case of the baptism-by-heretic? Is the possibility of a valid Eucharist not as much of a case of what is vital for salvation as baptism (if one follows the New Testament), a celebration to which baptized Christians even have a right? Should such a possibility not be tacitly recognized as arising from the nature of the church and therefore be explicitly recognized? If in "normal" cases of ecclesial celebrations of the Eucharist, their valid reality rests on the will, which the church itself provides (in ordination—or better, the habitual recognition of the priest by the church, if also according to the normal rules of ordination), why should it be beyond its power to set and manifest this will in a different way and thereby to provide that legal reality in a dimension that is much closer to itself, and much less separated from itself, than that in which the baptizing pagan or even the baptizing heretic does? For the church considers these circumstances as occurring in bad faith (*malae fidei*) and yet recognizes the ability to baptize.

Regarding the second objection (*too much*), one might say that according to the estimation of the church, the commissionability of baptism must, or at least can, be granted to the pagan,[3] evidently so that the salvation of as many as possible can be assured in a sacramental manner through this most fundamental sacrament. The authorization to celebrate Eucharist, however, has a different, collective, and (as a celebration of the assembly) intraecclesial character, so that the one entrusted with it seems more in need of having a greater closeness to the dimension that ultimately bears such authority. In any case, it is understandable why, in this case, the church has never thought beyond the dimension of baptized Christians. Moreover, it must not be overlooked that a concrete celebration of the Eucharist presupposes a multitude of celebrants, but in such a case, at any rate, at least one Christian must be presupposed. The argument would prove, at best, that where several Christians wish to celebrate the Eucharist, without *any* ordained minister of any church being present, a sacramental event would nevertheless come about through the Christian presiding over such a celebration. Of course, this is only where such a celebration of the Eucharist constitutes an emergency that could not have been otherwise resolved and not merely an arbitrary violation of the ordination requirement for normal cases. I do not understand why one should have to deny the sacramentality of such a celebration in such a case. There would not be the *ausus proprius* (proper intention), because of

---

3. SW has *Helden* (hero), although the sense of the sentence requires *Heiden*.

which "Mysterium ecclesiae," in the sixth chapter, denies (rightly) validity to eucharistic celebrations without ordained priests.[4,i]

The problem of "lay confession" in the Middle Ages is also reminiscent in this context.[j] Before Scotus, there existed among theologians the impression (though with variations and denials from some individuals) that one could and must confess to a layperson if one were in danger of death and did not have access to a priest and that this confession was then more or less sacramental. (Especially since you can hardly justify the obligation of making such a confession otherwise.) Even if, following Thomas Aquinas, this lay confession is called *quodammodo sacramentalis* (in some sense sacramental), one cannot say that Thomas simply denies that it is sacramental, even if it is not a "perfect sacrament." For if lay confession is not a sacrament in the usual official[5] clear sense, and *in this sense* is therefore not a "complete" sacrament, it is also not merely nothing. And therefore, it is, for Thomas, sacramental in some sense (*quodammodo*). Thomas would not have had to write in so cumbersome of a manner if his had just been the usual contemporary view. And so before Scotus, one did not reject such auxiliary help, which at that time would be quite theologically understandable (because such a justification was known to have been normal before priestly absolution had become standard). In any case, one would be justified by a completely

---

4. Rahner here refers to the Congregation for the Doctrine of the Faith's "Declaration in Defense of the Catholic Doctrine on the Church against Certain Errors of the Present Day,"—"Mysterium ecclesiae," Declaration, June 24, 1973—specifically paragraph 6, which says, "Passing over at this point questions regarding the ministers of various sacraments, the evidence of Sacred Tradition and of the sacred Magisterium make it clear that the faithful who have not received priestly ordination and who take upon themselves the office of performing the Eucharist attempt to do so not only in a completely illicit way but also invalidly." *Ausus proprius* here refers to the idea of the laity "taking upon themselves" the office of the priest.

5. "Office-ial"—that is, *Amtlich*.

extrasacramental "perfect" remorse, and so it was possible in such an emergency to postpone the sacrament until later, if that was possible. And so one did not merely see a dichotomy of either a sacrament under the totally normal official constraints and constitution *or* a merely "subjective" attainment of grace. In such emergencies, one sought a mediator and mediation. And so one was also ready to consider as such those who would be extraordinary and would not usually be considered as entering into the standard sacramental process. Is such a thing simply outdated by the "progress" of theology, or are we dealing today with an archaizing simplification that, for the sake of clarity and unambiguity, does not want to reckon with such extraordinary possibilities of sacramentality? Is such a thing as sacramental lay confession now only conceivable in the sense that medieval theology considered it?

In thinking about the sacrament of confession, we might also consider the so-called general absolution that, according to recent Roman teaching, is possible in various situations where individual confession is not feasible and that *is* a sacrament. One might naturally say that such a thing is possible precisely because, in the concrete situation, more is not possible. That a sacrament must be able to be administered because "the sacraments are intended for humans, and not humans for the sacraments" and because otherwise people may have to do without sacramental justification. But why then not also say in this case, "That doesn't work," because individual confession belongs to the nature of this sacrament; for the human being, the *votum sacramenti* and perfect contrition remain; even a sacrament is not "more secure" than the penitent's part that consists of the subjective return to God in repentance; a perfect contrition is therefore not more difficult than imperfect and without it the sacrament cannot be fruitful? Does not the difficulty of perfect contrition lie precisely in "imperfect" contrition—that is, in the honest turning away from one's sins? Even if this objection to the urgency of such general absolution is in itself rightly justified, one will make no objection to these general absolutions. But they demonstrate once again what flexibility the effective word of forgiveness in the mouth of the church can have. And ought one not then doubt that this flexibility must absolutely end precisely where in the practice of today's church it in fact does?

5

Form, Validity, and History

Yet one more consideration should be made explicit in order to round out our theological "exercises" (in order to speak with Origen). We have looked at the great variability of the various sacramental signs, which did not do damage to the continuity of their graceful operation. One can demonstrate a similar variability in each of the other sacraments. There is baptism by immersion, by infusion, and by submersion. We do not know definitively if the anointing or the laying on of hands is decisive in confirmation.

Regarding confirmation, we traditionally say that its "ordinary" minister is the bishop. According to recent Roman decrees, however, every priest who baptizes adults may immediately confirm them.[a] If one considers that adult baptism is actually the normative case (theologically understood, rather than in terms of the current ecclesial-sociological situation), then one must therefore ask if, speaking theologically, the common priest does not become the ordinary minister of the sacrament. And perhaps if someday, should adult baptism become the norm also in the common consciousness, then perhaps these two sacraments, baptism and confirmation, will (again in the common conception) more or less become *one* sacrament of initiation. This wouldn't be terrible. This consideration demonstrates just how "fluid," how dependent on the will of the church, the entire matter of sacraments is even today.

One can receive the Eucharist under one or both species. There is both public and private absolution, given under indicative or subjunctive form.[1] Anointing of the sick can be celebrated by anointing the forehead or the particular parts of the body. The solemnization of the marriage declaration can occur in various forms, including representation by a proxy. Ordination has been understood to occur through the *traditio instrumentorum*, or through the laying on of hands, or by both. Now, people had good reasons for all of these variations. If one looks at them more carefully, however, one notices that these reasons were only convincing because people had liturgically acted in just such a way previously and were used to these practices, and these only later received a reflective justification. Such and such a practice was customary and therefore the reasons subsequently brought to light would be obvious to those considering them. If, for example, there were no communion under a single kind, I should like to see the theologian who would not find the currently ubiquitous arguments against communion under one kind to be obvious. Why—using proofs from Scriptures and ancient practice—should *wheat* bread be necessary matter, but not the double species in the individual's communion? If marriage were not allowed to have been solemnized via a proxy, then any theologian would probably say—with a clean theological conscience—that while one could, of course, conclude any contract through a proxy, the sacramental nature of marriage forbids such a form because no one can receive a sacrament at a distance, just as no one could be given an absolution by a voice transmitted via satellite.[2]

---

1. He is referring here to the possibility of "absolvo te," versus "indulgeat tibi Dominus."

2. The recent experience of socially distanced and virtual liturgy in the time of Covid-19 has prompted new thinking about "sacraments at a distance," including quite a few early-pandemic reflections on the usefulness and limitations of notions of "spiritual communion." While to my knowledge, these have mostly existed in blogs and diocesan newspapers, it would not be surprising if Rahner's point about

The strangeness of this variation of the sacraments continues to lie in the fact that it has not only developed in a most unreflective manner but also does not reveal any clear principle according to which this variability originated or is legitimized. Why for example, is an anointing of the sick invalid if oil is used that was not blessed for that purpose by the bishop?[3] Why must the eucharistic bread absolutely be made of wheat? After all, one can only transcend all these difficulties (including the establishment of all the sacraments by Jesus) and get past all the oppressive individual justifications if one simply and courageously says that the sacraments (in light of all the historical connections of such sacramental acts, as described above, to the historical Jesus) are articulations of the fundamental nature of the church toward the individual in their existentially significant situation. The sacraments thus have their nature and their origin in Jesus Christ and, therefore, to a much greater extent, are at the disposal of the church. In beginning thus, the particular historical variations of sacramental distribution can thus be disregarded, as the factual and reflexive scope of these variations does not define the extent to which such variation is fundamentally possible. Such is presumably, for example, also the case for sacramental ordination in the Middle Ages, in which the lower orders were regarded as sacraments, and therefore (should we not say?) they also really *were* greater than they are today. We acknowledge only three "grades" of ordination and *therefore* that is all we have.

---

the variability of sacramental practice in light of need (and its later theological explanation) would mean that in the years to come, new theological proposals about spiritual communion and liturgy in the technological era develop.

3. Perhaps strengthening Rahner's point here are the changes made to canon law regarding the sacrament of extreme unction / anointing of the sick. Cf. CIC 1917 can. 945 and CIC 1983 can. 999. The former allows the oil to be blessed by a bishop or a presbyter with faculties from the Holy See, whereas the 1983 code allows any presbyter to bless the oil within the celebration of the rite "in case of necessity" (can. 999, 2°).

Today, as we have a greater possibility for reflecting on the church's actual past behavior regarding the sacraments, we should, without bias and with practical courage, expect there to be more variety in the sacramental event, whether it is explicitly acknowledged or not. If we insist that every marriage contracted between baptized persons is a sacrament, even if the spouses absolutely do not know and do not want to know anything about this, then we are also thereby saying that sacramental events occur within the church and because of it, of which neither the church (in the concrete sense) nor the sacramental ministers know anything. Why shouldn't there be other similar such cases? Could not Christian religious rites in the dimension, or arising from it, in which the separated churches are nevertheless united mean that they have a sacramental character arising from the foundational nature of the church, even if such a church should not know anything at all about this explicitly? Even if that church does not adequately conform to the normal explicit conditions for the validity of the sacraments? Provided only that they do not deny such a character of this religious event to others. If, through bona fides and a salvific faith, they are connected with the church and they cannot be seriously asked to conform to the normative form of this religious rite (even if they continually live under the obligation to "regularize" this religious activity so that it also corresponds to those norms that are explicitly required by the church for the validity of sacraments in the normal case, so that their public disregard must be presumed to constitute *malae fidei*), must this practice invalidate these rites sacramentally?

Here and there, in this complex of questions, we have invoked the concept of the *oikonomia* in Eastern theology. One could then object again that the concept, where and how it actually occurs, does not apply to our question. Can one suppose that our considerations contain hints on how to give this concept a theological foundation and a theological weight so that it can also be applied to our fundamental question? One certainly does not have a theological definition if they merely think that God is content to leave well enough alone when there isn't another option.[4]

Here we will end our theological speculation.[5] Truly, I wanted only to pose some questions and demonstrate that much more is unclear than is sometimes assumed by a too settled and positivist theology. These considerations are such that should someone wish to, should they be too certain of their own traditional opinion from the outset, they only too easily can assert that everything here is all muddled up[6] and therefore that I have "proven" nothing. Whoever thinks this should, in my opinion, search their own conscience and determine if it is important to them that the work for the unification of the churches progress concretely or whether they are only giving it lip service because speaking in this way is considered to be good manners in the church today. I am only posing questions. But they are questions that should be seriously considered. Even if you approve in general of their goal, which was quite plain, many more questions, of course, remain that were not touched upon. Not only is this work lacking important historical and systematic arguments (as was already stipulated at the beginning), but there are also a number of distinctions that would be important to make. For, of course, it should not be asserted that any particular act in any Christian denomination that has any affinity with the Catholic sacraments should necessarily be recognized as a sacrament or that any permanent function in any Christian denomination is already a ministry within the meaning of order transmitted in the Catholic Church through a sacramental ordination. Here I have only asked questions, and very general ones at that. But one *is* still permitted to ask.

---

4. *Der liebe Gott werde schon fünfe grad sein lassen, wenn es nicht anders geht.*

5. Rahner is once again returning to the metaphor of "ein Fahrt ins Blaue"—a Sunday drive, an experiment.

6. *Ist wie Kraut und Rüben durcheinander.*

6

Bearing Our Divisions
on the Way to Unity

My considerations had come thus far and I had intended to stop there. But I gave the text to a theologian in whose knowledge and personal understanding I had great confidence. He thought that I should add a conclusion to the project (which he endorsed, even in its more aporetic form) to systematically summarize and expressly state the most important conclusions of what has been said. In response to such a request, I have no objections so long as the aporetic character of the entire deliberation is not obscured by further words giving the reader the impression that all the data necessary for forming an accurate opinion on the question of ministry in today's situation have been taken into account. That is not the case (as I said at the beginning) because I have not completed all the biblical, dogmatic, and doctrinal examinations that would be necessary for such a final judgment. If, however, no summary, "synthetic" basic judgment on the question of ministry can be offered, and if providing one is fundamentally impossible here, my colleague's expressed wish for a conclusion is not simply meaningless. It can be understood as a request to clarify once again what will emerge from the various considerations regarding a basic agreement on the ecclesiastical ministry once other, heretofore omitted and yet much more fundamental (i.e., exegetical and church-doctrinal) reflections have been made. And to show that this will not necessarily contradict the overall result of these considerations so far. Subject to the proviso that this summary remains a permanently aporetic "systematization," I would like to try to respond to my colleague's request. If in doing so, one or the other thought should emerge that has not yet been expressly considered, it seems to me that this would not speak against this "synthesis" but for it.

The church is the "Sacrament for the Healing of the World." This is expressed everywhere both piously and insistently. And this adage must intend to speak of a "world" that is not simply equivalent with the church but external, historically and sociologically considered, which stands outside of it. Otherwise, the sentence would be tautological: the church is (in its corporate-historical realm) the sign of that healing that takes place within it. The church must also be a sign of healing for the world outside of it, for the entire world and for all of history. It is self-evident that it is not and cannot be a sign of salvation in this world that is expressly recognized as such, because otherwise this world would no longer be "outside of the church." It must, if the sentiment is to have any real meaning, have to do with being an "effective sign." If this were not the case, then one could only explain this symbolic character of the church, its being a sign of the salvation of the world, as a *declaration* that the world is so ruled by God's saving purpose that even people who do not belong to it deserve salvation and can and will obtain it. Such a declaration is traceable back to its essence. In its being, however, the church is the sacrament of the world's healing. Otherwise, the church would be proclaiming a salvation for the non-Christian world that would not actually belong to it; the axiom *extra ecclesiam nulla salus* would have lost its acknowledged *universal* and *positive* meaning. It simply has to be this way: because and in so far as the truly effective self-communication of God in the Spirit (as faith, hope, and love) is always and everywhere the innermost entelechy of world history, salvation is possible everywhere *and* the church is the historical tangibility of this saving will of God and its irreversibility in Christ, the crucified and risen Lord, as the congregation of faith in this eschatological event. The church therefore has an eschatologically peculiar sign-character. I say *sign* because it is a sign that occurs, and this sign is not only an afterthought of the signified, but an *effective* sign, because the signing takes place within its historical tangibility. At the same time, the complexity of the church's reality should not be overlooked: it is the presence of the world-conquering, saving Spirit *and* the corporate historical tangibility of this (word- and sacrament-related) presence of the Spirit in the world. These moments are neither identical nor merely separable; they have however, especially if the church is to be the sacrament of the healing of the *world*, a graduated, variable relationship to each other that does not simply cease to exist where the church (in a purely corporate sense) "ends," but continues on past every such border. Otherwise, the salvation of all persons through the church; baptism by an unbaptized person, the testimony of faith by a "martyr" who has not yet been baptized; the *hearing* of the Scripture by one still unbaptized, which is nevertheless heard as the word of God in the Spirit (i.e., more than the sermon itself); the experience of the Spirit of Mercy and the testimony about it; and other such events "outside" the church would be inconceivable. Whoever, along with Vatican II, counts the self-donation of God in the Spirit as being part of what is constitutive of the church (in correction to the Bellarmanian definition of *church*), for this person, the full societal (hierarchical) form of the church does not exist everywhere, but they still cannot name everything that is done outside of the "church" (in this strong, societal sense of the episcopal-papal structure) as being "non-Catholic" (although grace-filled). Where there is grace, there also is the church, even if also in various levels of tangibility and expression. To deny this would be to fall back into an outdated theology of the church in which the Spirit does not belong to the being of the church, or else presupposes the opinion that such a Spirit only had a connection then and there, but not universally, to its historical-societal appearances in the ecclesial. Insofar as this Spirit belongs only to the church and is *nevertheless* universally operative wherever salvation occurs, one can say that the church (as a unity of Spirit and sign) has "radiated" and, by this radiation, is also verifiable and tangible because of its effects, even if it is not operating in its full corporate and historical structure. Such a thing might seem difficult to grasp and yet more difficult to describe. But this difficulty can only be remedied if one is willing to give up either the idea that the church is necessary for salvation or the universal offer of salvation (including to those "outside" the church), or if one attempts to reconcile them too easily (e.g., the appeal to a purely "existential" and "private" desire that replaces the church with the desire for church, one that is wholly "implicit" in the consciousness of humanity as such, not merely existing, but merely interpretative). This radiative power, which results from its essence (that is, Spirit), cannot annul the church at all, nor "delimit" it by an arbitrary decree. The church is the sacrament of the healing of the world, and it must be that. Through a more exact consideration, one might show that every act of healing, wherever it takes place "outside" the church, makes a historically viable and social location to be "ecclesial" in the broadest sense (because, in a metaphysical-anthropological sense, there can be no purely "inner" and "private" acts, and therefore any division between human actions of this kind is empirically sensible but of a purely secondary nature). For there, the power of the Spirit of God lets itself be experienced in history—that Spirit who finds its complete manifestation in what one usually calls the church.

All this holds true all the more, and in a very specific and qualitative sense, when something "outside" the church is ecclesiastical in the narrower sense (the existence and proclamation of the written word of God, sacramental signs that at least desire to be sacraments of Christ, occurrences in which Christians at least desire to organize themselves as Christian communities, etc.). These *are* truly ecclesial, if also in varying degrees and a variety of ways.

One cannot absolutely refuse such things the descriptor "church" if the Roman Catholic Church applies the predicate "ecclesial" to these societies into which they happen. And when and where it does not wish to apply the description of "church" to one of these communities, for whatever reason (*Lumen gentium* §15), it then names them "communitates ecclesiasticae."[a] Even in such cases, therefore, it has no objection to the term "ecclesial." "Church" and "ecclesial" cannot be understood as general concepts that name a multipliable, sociological-historical content that empirically exists in different socializations as such, nor can these concepts be understood to be so used in *Lumen gentium* (at least alone) because these communities have even granted these terms and peacefully adapted to this language use. Finally "church" and "ecclesial" are words that describe something of which there is, and can be, only one. So also concerning the impact of that communication to the world of the Spirit of God, this Spirit's effects wherever they occur in historical-social form, are "ecclesial." These effects can have a variety of grades and intensities (this is also true within the Catholic Church: the first proclamation, for example, of the word of God, up to the Eucharist, or the full expression of ministry in the church in the various hierarchical levels). Such ecclesial realities should not be called "ecclesial" if they were concluded by individuals through their own guilt in setting these realities against the historical-social presence of the saving Spirit of Christ in the world in which all such moments are gathered (at least in principle) and that we Catholics in the Catholic Church recognize—including their Episcopal and Petrine constitution. There, however, where such exists, even if they are partial in comparison to the whole, insofar as they demonstrate the effects of the Spirit (up to an actually organized social structure), if they exist without constituting a "no" to the *whole* church (i.e., a "no" that is culpable or exists in situations of human action that must be presumed to be culpable), there exists a piece of the one, singular church and not a separate church, which would constitute two or more churches in the plural. To affirm the opposite of this would require that one denies either that this reality is a creation of the Spirit (or could be such)—and who would possibly say this still today in the age of ecumenism?—or that the one Spirit, through all of his expressions and presences in history, pushes on toward the *one* church.

In this view, we have by no means adopted that theory rejected by the Catholic magisterium, according to which the one church consists of simply the many churches as equal parts or the branches of a tree. If only because then the unity of the church would no longer have to be achieved or at most would be a secular-sociological question that does not touch upon the theological nature of the church. And the opinion implied here is precisely that the one Spirit may indeed (according to a providence of God, which must first be accepted as a fact, and that, where it is not a question of guilt, would necessarily be understood positively and not merely as an allowance for weakness) first of all create its societal-historical self-presence in the world and has nevertheless not yet reached full unity. But of course this is true because one wants to unite these various presences into a single church-corporate unity, which is the object of this divine providence (in unforeseeable times and ways) as well as the task of Christians who, being moved at different points of humanity and its history by this one Spirit and already recognizing and acknowledging this Spirit as the Spirit of Jesus, already form a piece of the church and act ecclesially. Because the actual guilt of the divisions presupposed in the earlier action is not ours today and can no longer really be judged by us (neither as an anticipation of the judgment of God, which is self-evident, nor in the way in which at the beginning of the split people could not avoid making such a judgment because they had to act in one way or the other). We in our times do not presume mutual guilt in the continuation of the divide—because we must be aligned with the future of the church (otherwise we would have to despair and act as those who only wait for the Lord's return). Therefore, the "division" must be theologically interpreted as pointing away from the present to the future. But then one can say, without further ado, that the Spirit of God, everywhere in the world, forms and has formed the church, which God continues to move on the way to full unity. But in this, no "equal rights" are claimed between these "ecclesial realities."[1] Such a thing is also not simply assumed by the various Protestant and Orthodox churches, if they take their own confessions seriously. Thus, if the Catholic Church regards the episcopate and the Petrine ministry in a historically tangible legitimate (apostolic) succession, as belonging to the fullness of the church, then it will declare a doctrine that will contradict other Christianities, but it does not formally do anything different from what other Christians do when they live in "separated" churches and do not regard this separateness as a merely historical—that is, as a theologically and spiritually irrelevant—contingency.

Therefore, if there are ministries and actions that at least desire to be sacramental (though perhaps without using the word itself) in these "separate" churches, why shouldn't they, or how could they not be, regarded as occurrences and realities, in or by which the Spirit of God is active (which today no one any longer categorically denies) but also as works *of* this Spirit (ordered toward unity)? But if this is true, then, why shouldn't these ministries be viewed generally as legitimate (with the qualification of their being ordered to the unity and the integration of the entire one, also Petrine, church)? Why should actions that intend to be sacramental and to be accompanied by the Spirit (and which are effected as such) not be regarded as sacramental? If, nevertheless, one does not want to call them sacramental, because they do not have full unity with the whole of the ecclesiastical spiritual presence in its corporate dimension, then one presupposes something that would have to be proved. Namely, that the recognition of a sacrament can only occur through an ecclesiastical recognition of the work of the Spirit (by means of an explicit act) and not by an implicit acknowledgment (whether always given

---

1. *Kirchlichkeiten*.

or merely possible). Otherwise one makes this language and the definition of terms above to be finally arbitrary, about which it would not be worthwhile to argue in the first place. And then it must be seriously asked whether such a regulation of language ought not be rejected, not because it is impossible and false in itself, but because it unduly obscures facts that are more important than the sharpening of the (in itself correct) demand that ministries and signs of grace, which are works of the Spirit, should also be in fully manifest relationships to those moments that we Catholic Christians believe belong to the complete constitution of the church. And never let it be forgotten in such considerations that it cannot and it must not be denied that the Spirit of God has brought these realities into being precisely because they had become detached in the past from the full unity of spiritual presence in the world, which never should have happened (whether or not there is guilt on both sides or either). We also cannot deny that these present realities have a historical connection with this earlier reality. Because the one Spirit causes all these realities (both graces and ministries), albeit in a "scattered" way, and in a certain sense—while they are still separate (though with an interior dynamic toward a full unity)—may one not yet say that they are effected as such by the Spirit?

And so why shouldn't such ministries and signs of grace not be able to be called legitimate? That they are in a condition of not yet having achieved the fullness of their own being in the realm of the corporate and ecclesiastically tangible is undisputed within Christianity, insofar as this recognizes the full unity of Christians as a still unfulfilled task for the churches. The only thing that is debated is what this full unity will look like according to the will of Christ and of God. But at least this division and the condition of not yet having achieved the fullness of the church's own being needn't be presumed to be blameworthy. In practice, it isn't (at least as far as the ecclesiastical and social dimensions are concerned). And so there is no reason not to acknowledge these realities as spiritually effective and therefore to call them legitimate and sacramental. One must not overlook the fact that even something importune (from the perspective of God's will) can be of various kinds. Something that is directly culpable against God's will and commandments is a very different kind of thing than things about which this cannot be said, even if they are also importune. Whether something that ought not be the case mediates the culpability of the historical fault or simply remains as an imperfection to be overcome in the future (i.e., according to the historically becoming character of the human being), such "importune" actualities may even be positively intended by God so that they can be understood as having been acts of God in accordance with their particular nature. (Our death, for example, is understood to have arisen from original sin and, from this perspective, is something that should not have happened, but it can and must be understood as something positively enacted by God and therefore as being, in a positive sense, a gift.)

All of our considerations to this point have proceeded from a specifically Catholic viewpoint and Catholic assumptions. The Protestant Christian and theologian might therefore have the impression not only that, because it wrestles with requirements that they do not share, this text has been laboriously seeking to understand and justify the legitimacy of their ministries and sacraments, but also that it is attempting to "appropriate" their ministry and sacraments for the Catholic Church, an attempt to which the Protestant must strenuously reject.[2] Last but not least, one must again say something about this conceivable misgiving.

---

2. Precisely this claim was made about the *Joint Declaration on the Doctrine of Justification* in an open letter from 141 German Protestant professors of theology in 1998. See "Votum der Hochschullehrer zur 'Gemeinsamen Erklärung zur Rechtfertigungslehre,'" in *Die Gemeinsame Erklärung zur Rechtfertigungslehre: Dokumentation des Entstehungs und Rezeptionsprozesses*, ed. Friedrich Hauschild, Udo Hahn, and Andreas Siemens (Göttingen: Vandenhoeck & Ruprecht, 2009), document C.27.b. Also see my *Mapping the Differentiated Consensus of the Joint Declaration* (New York: Palgrave, 2016), 26–28.

First of all, as far as the first part of this question is concerned, if and to the extent that the theologies of the separate churches still differ from one another, it is entirely unavoidable and must not be cause for blame by the other side that each attempts to understand the reality and self-understanding of the other church beginning from one's own point of view. This, of course, happens on the basis of assumptions that the other side does not share and that therefore must seem to be cumbersome, laborious, and tricky means by which to prove things, because what is self-evident (for the other side) is not self-evident for the first and therefore requires justification. There is no cure for this so long as the parties are not explicitly and clearly unified in all of their basic assumptions. Each side must have patience with the other when one feels the attempt at bridging from the other side to be cumbersome while still feeling carefree standing on the right side of the divide. Naturally, a Protestant Christian will approach their own Eucharist as a self-evidently valid and legitimate fulfillment of Jesus's charge and as a reality regarding which there is really nothing worth fighting about. But for the Catholic, this does not arise naturally from their assumptions, and they must first pave the way for themselves by a long process of reflection in which their own presuppositions remain valid and must be made fruitful for this new question before they can then proceed along this road toward a positive appraisal of the conception of the Protestant Christian.

The second part of the objection (the accusation of a typically Catholic "appropriation") needs a somewhat more detailed engagement. It is clear and must first of all be accepted as a fact by the Protestant Christian that in a Catholic understanding of the church the Petrine ministry and episcopal structure belong to the full essence of the church of Christ and that according to this same understanding of the Roman Catholic Church, there are no moments in which they are lacking. They must belong to the church of Christ in an organizational way, and so such moments (where they are lacking) would be absolutely excluded from the Catholic Church according to its own self-understanding. In this sense, according to the Catholic understanding, the church of Christ "subsists" in the Roman Catholic Church. This position, of course, does not include the assertion that every moment in which the church of Christ should be explicitly existing in the Catholic Church is in history sufficiently clear, explicit, and historically tangible and better than any other church. That is, that in achieving agreement with other churches, it would not be more so the church of Christ, but only quantitatively larger. If the churches and therefore also the Roman Catholic Church came into full unity, the Catholic Church would also receive a fuller expression of her own being and, in this sense, would become a new, different church. In that sense, then, in which it stands as *the* church, in which the church of Christ "subsists," it cannot fail to refer everything that is Christian in the world to itself, to regard them as elements that have an inner tendency, also historically and tangibly within themselves, and these elements aim toward the church of the future, of which it is an anticipation, and into which they will be integrated. Naturally, this is a confessional point of dissention for Protestant theology, even if it must be more exactly formulated than can be done here. But this has nothing to do with a "reception of other churches" by the Catholic Church.

The reason is apparently simple: Ultimately, all our considerations were based on the Spirit of God finally and victoriously communicated to the world through the Christ event; through this communication a reality exists in the world, by which the solution of all questions of ministry and sacrament no longer consist merely in the postulate of a will and decree of God, through which—in a hidden way on God's side—he is willing to give grace where sacraments, ministries, and churches do not exist, or do not exist legitimately. This Spirit effects itself, according to Catholic ecclesial understanding, and is available (in a particular respect) as fully present in the world historically, institutionally, and sacramentally through the Catholic Church, but God himself effects the other Christians in the world and in the churches themselves. He dynamically directs this toward the one church of the future, which, according to Catholic conviction, will also be the episcopal and Petrine Roman Catholic Church, which, in a legitimate succession, will go back to the first church. But the Spirit has an effect on this extra-Catholic Christian that (always under the self-evident condition that this dynamic is oriented toward the future church) is ecclesiastical, legitimate, and therefore also Catholic. There is a relationship that is analogous to the relationship that exists among the sacraments administered within the Catholic Church: because they are "pneumatic" (at least in being the word of an offer of grace to human freedom, for example, in a *sacramentum validum, etsi infructuosum*), they are also ecclesial, and not just vice versa: because they are ecclesial, they are also pneumatic, graceful. This second foundational relationship also exists. The first is clearly the primary one, precisely because the saving will of God in God's pneumatic self-donation to the world primarily causes the reality of Christ being in the world—although one can also say that because Christ is, grace is in the world. The second relationship cannot be denied unless one wishes to rob the sacraments of their effectiveness ("instrumentality" or however this is termed). But this second relationship (grace *because* of sacraments and church) may not be allowed to cancel out or deny the first, or it will be founded only in itself. How to preserve and understand the second while preserving the first is still not entirely clear but it might provide a glimpse into an improved Catholic sacramental theology that better describes the effectiveness and mode of the sacraments. Even in Thomas, the matter is not entirely clear.

The best way to say it is this: the effectiveness of the sacraments (and, let us add, *mutatis mutandis*, the legitimacy of office) is ultimately the effectiveness of the "sign" as such. The efficacy of the sacraments is not a peculiarity of the sacrament, which stands *in addition to* its sign-character, but the self-efficacy given in this character itself. Grace is effected by the sign, and insofar as it creates its historical-social ecclesial presence as its own manifestation, is effected by having its presence in the dimension of history and of the church. If and insofar as there are also legitimate ministries and valid sacraments "outside of" the Catholic Church, they are not coopted by this concrete church, but it is instead said that these offices and sacraments are historical-ecclesiastical embodiments of the Spirit and have an inner ordering from this Spirit toward the church, according to the Catholic understanding of the church as the "full" embodiment of this Spirit. Wherever it blows, it creates ecclesiality. Even if it is now still scattered, it is directed toward that full unity toward which all ecclesiality is aligned and moves. If the Protestant Christian and theologian is convinced of the importance of this yet-to-be achieved *unitary* church, and also recognizes valid ministry and right sacramental administration, does not see in it merely a "synagogue of Satan," then he cannot think otherwise in the last word about this scattered ecclesiastical tradition, even though he thinks that in this unified church, these ecclesiastical structures need not be given a Petrine and episcopal structure, as they must according to Catholic ways of thinking. Therefore, if in the theory presented here, a Protestant theologian wanted to see an unseemly "appropriation" of his ministries and sacraments by the Catholic Church, then it would have to be said that he cannot do otherwise than to do the same thing in reverse if he believes in the *one* church (whether as a present or future reality) and grants that something genuinely ecclesial exists in the Catholic Church. For if we want to speak in terms of an "appropriation," then at most the question can be who legitimately appropriates whom.

Appendix

An Excursus on Intercommunion

Methodology

1. The question of intercommunion engages a very complex reality. The church; her ministers; her believers with their wide complexity and variety of levels of belief and ecclesial belonging; the members of other Christian confessions, churches, and ecclesial communities; the sacramental acts in their various dimensions; the private and ecclesial natures of the event of salvation; and many other aspects relate to this question of intercommunion. In addition, it is difficult to say how binding (in a theological sense) the practices and decisions of the church of times past are on this question, especially since the question can always be raised (for all matters relating to the sacraments) as to whether a church norm concerning the sacraments *presupposes* or *creates* a sacramental state of affairs. It is precisely the ecclesial-social aspect of the sacrament that, as social, is such that its sense, legitimacy, and weight are determined by assumptions and horizons that are not reflected upon in the standard sacramental theology but are constitutive for the meaning and legitimacy of the sacrament even though they can go unnoticed in the historical process. Therefore, the old norms on the sacramental practice must always be revised, even if the "substance" of the

sacraments must always be preserved. After all, one would always have to reconsider the question of the meaning of the sacraments from the vantage point of a clarified concept of what revelation really is, and it would then prove once again that there is much *more* actual authority given to the church than one usually thinks, and thus much is fundamentally changeable, even if one may have to reckon with the fact that previous decisions of the church in the field of the sacraments, though once contingent, later become irreversible.[a]

2. Given what has just been said, it seems methodologically appropriate, and really to be the only approach that is likely to produce results, if one starts considering the question of intercommunion by beginning with the present practices of the church. Otherwise, one is in the highest danger going forward of making ideological premises that basically presuppose only one answer to the question that has been posed. If one is tacitly convinced of the correctness of their conclusion, just as too often happens in much of moral theology, one subsequently yields a speculative justification of a proposition of which one is already convinced, with the assertion that the argumentation is certain and would produce the opinion in question even if one were not already convinced that it is correct. Of course, calling on the practice of the church today is also a somewhat problematic and dangerous endeavor. For, as history has shown, one can certainly not rule out a priori that there have been many abuses and aberrations in the practice of the church, some of which have even been legislated and institutionalized. On the other hand, however, there is a twofold point to be kept in mind: it is indeed the case that the social practice of the church is constitutive of much of the meaning and significance of such a sign—that is, these signs are not merely the realization of an unchangeable being coming from revelation alone. This fact, which in principle cannot be denied,

greatly diminishes the danger that the practice of the church will do something inimical to its being in this area. It should also be borne in mind that in practice the church acts, at least in its most important supreme representatives, from a global, more unreflective preconception that has at least as much—yes, more—weight than the preconceptions of the individual theologian who might argue against this practice, which regardless of whether they admit it or not, reflect on it or not, must work within their theological reasoning.

3. Thus, in spite of all objections, we have the theological right to proceed from contemporary church practice and to presuppose, in this question, that what the church does is in fact also theologically legitimately done by it. Such a presumption cannot, however, be extended evenly to all the details of this practice. It is quite possible that among the practical individual norms that are issued by the church on our question, there are tensions. Yes, perhaps even contradictions, which cannot be speculatively resolved, but simply must be acknowledged with the demand for a better standardization without such contradictions. So we are only assuming that on the whole this practice bears a true legitimacy. Such a limited presumption is also important in our question, for it may well be, according to the indications given, that in certain cases, the church prohibits intercommunion of a particular kind, although it *must* or at least *could* be permitted if it remained consistently faithful to those inner principles, which the church tacitly recognizes in those other cases in which it does allow for intercommunion.

4. The method to be followed here is, nevertheless, not merely a reference to the church's concrete norms for action on this question or their merely external systematization. Rather, it is a matter of questioning these norms on the principles that are, albeit without clear reflection, embodied in them, thus reducing these factual norms to an ultimately clear

and illuminating principle, and from there once again asking whether such a principle, if applied correctly, does not also yield further concrete norms of action for other circumstances.

Current Church Norms on Intercommunion

1. For practical reasons, we treat only the admission of non-Catholic Christians to full participation in the Catholic Eucharist.

2. The existing norms on this question can be reduced (with sufficient precision for our purposes) to the following general propositions:

   a. The church rejects a general and unconditional admission of non-Catholic Christians, even when they are baptized, to full eucharistic communion, before they have become members of the Catholic Church in a legally tangible manner as a single person or ecclesial group according to the principles that apply to full church membership. This basic norm is self-evident and needs no fuller justification. Full eucharistic fellowship, at least where it is fully enacted in the public sphere of the church and society at large, is also a result and a confession of full church membership in the Catholic Church. If we ignore the nuances of this principle in favor of a generalized formulation of the principle expressed in this norm, then Catholic theologians are probably all in agreement about it and also to the resulting consequences. Because of this at least operational unity on the teaching, the question of whether this norm is absolutely of divine law or demonstrates a certain amount of the influence of a positive determination on the part of the church need not be further asked here. For doubtless, in the second case too, the church would have the right to make such a determination as to when participation in her full eucharistic liturgy will be permitted, and there must be no doubt[b] about the appropriateness and purposefulness of such a possibly conceivable decision.

b. However, in certain cases, the church permits the admission of a non-Catholic Christian to receive the Eucharist as would be granted to a Catholic Christian. As I said before, we consider such "exceptions" to be legitimate, at least for the most part. Such exceptions are granted, even though those admitted might be mistaken in regard to a Catholic dogma on, for example, papal primacy and full episcopal succession (hence also in the dimension of *potestas iurisdictionis*) and without having repudiated this error. And therefore, to put it simply, the question of whether a difference of opinion regarding the dogma of the Eucharist itself makes an intercommunion impossible is not obviously or simply answered. But this must be dealt with later. In any case, however, these church-approved "exceptions" already demonstrate that not every case of a difference of faith or being divided from the church (however this may be conceived) means being forbidden admission to the Catholic Eucharist. Therefore, it can only be a question of our discerning principles by which these extant norms can be understood as forming a meaningful unity within the double character that we have just established governs the church's action.

Principles Embedded in These Norms

1. If a legitimate intercommunion exists, there must certainly be (for both the Catholics and the non-Catholics who are partaking), a certain sameness of action both objectively and in some subjective sense. This principle is usually presumed to be tacitly taken for granted. But it is better to say

it explicitly. When human beings come together in a common action, they have to strive to act in common if they are to act properly. In considering the essential moments of the sacraments, in which the objective validity and the subjective appropriation and "fruitfulness" are not simply identical, one must consider this required sameness of action in intercommunion on the part of the Catholic and non-Catholic sides in its both objective and subjective aspects. Regarding the objective aspect, there is not much to say in our case, as for the celebration of the Eucharist (about which we are thinking), this is fundamentally constituted by the validly ordained and legitimately called Catholic priest. With regard to the subjective side of this unity, from the point of view of the meaningfulness and moral legitimacy of a common human action, at minimum a very fundamental unity must be required. Where on the non-Catholic side, no religious action was intended at all, where it was clear that only a conventional bourgeois consideration should be considered to exist, such an intercommunion should be rejected from the standpoint of human decency. So the question can only be what sameness is required and what is not regarding the genuinely religious meaning of this common eucharistic celebration on the part of the non-Catholic partner with the Catholic community. That absolute sameness is not required is already established by the extant norms of the church. It would be too great a simplification of the question, if one wanted to respond to the matter, that with regard to the Eucharist itself, an absolute unity of belief would be required, but that this would not be necessary with regard to other beliefs. It is true that the question of the sameness of the conviction concerning the Eucharist therefore has a legitimate priority in our question because it has to do with the eucharistic communion, not any other communion in other acts of the church or of faith. But obviously, the solution just envisaged is too simple. If only because objectively and also typically subjectively the celebration of the Eucharist is the supreme making-present of this Catholic Church in the concreteness of its constitution and its faith. The eucharistic celebration in and of itself has very much to do with the whole of the Catholic faith and with the self-understanding of the church. The particular dogmas to some extent each interact with it. As an example, a Catholic eucharistic celebration always includes a commemoration of the pope and the bishop, so that the admission of an Orthodox Christian, as opposed to a Protestant Christian, does not solve the problem. But if there are any cases of intercommunion that do not only appear to be such (in which a complete membership of the non-Catholic Christian with the Catholic Church is actually achieved on the side of the non-Catholic and for which the non-Catholic has an explicit or implicit intent), and that are legitimate, then a full selfsameness of belief cannot be a prerequisite for any intercommunion to be legitimate. In this question there is also the difference between the conviction of faith as objectively given in the confession of one or another church, that is presupposed—usually too quickly and naively—as also being present in the individual members of the church concerned, and the actual understanding of faith in its usually limiting primitiveness, which actually exists among the individual members of the different churches. Where an intercommunion, for reasons that will be discussed later, is not a public demonstration to the churches and society of an already-existing communion in faith between the churches or of a complete indifference to the denominational differences in teaching, there need not be too great demands made regarding the subjective sameness of the beliefs of the two parties, especially in the subjective faith-consciousness of the ones making the intercommunion. There are not really many objectively existent differences of faith in the subjective consciousness, and therefore,[c] the objective differences of faith between the churches according to the practical norms of the church need not prohibit intercommunion so long as this does not constitute a demonstration of the irrelevance of these differences.

2. There exists a real difference (if one may say this) between the communal and private symbolism of the sacramental act. This real difference exists, and therefore, in principle, considering it is legitimate. Here we touch on a central point in the whole controversy concerning intercommunion. The rejection of intercommunion is usually explained by the fact that the Eucharist is not merely the sign of Christ's gracious gift to the individual for his salvation but also the sign of the unity of the church. Assuming that these two aspects of the Eucharist are simply and in every case of equal importance and could not be objectively differentiated from one another in any case, open communion would be in every case forbidden, because the ecclesial character of an open communion for the sake of completeness and clarity would not exist, although the private symbolic character is also present. But if there is any legitimate case of open communion, then these two symbolisms cannot be just two mirror-image versions of the same symbolism. So the question can only be what lack of ecclesiastical symbolism makes an open communion legitimate and which[d] not.

3. This question can certainly not be answered simply positivistically—that is, by saying that every open communion that has been expressly permitted by the church is not lacking the ecclesial symbolism that would forbid open communion, while all other cases have such a shortcoming. For the cases permitted by the church require an inner justification, even if it is assumed that for true legitimacy, an explicit permission on the part of the church must be added to this matter and that this positive permission is also required by

the matter itself. Moreover, beyond the cases explicitly permitted by the church, the church grants the possibility that
there may be other similar cases that are also legitimate, at
least given the consent of the bishop concerned. It therefore remains necessary to ask the question, Which are the
cases arising from the thing itself, in which an open communion is allowed, and in which not? It is therefore necessary to seek a fundamental demarcation that legitimizes the
de facto demarcation made by the church and is useful for
interpreting similar cases, without thereby legitimizing every
intercommunion.

We will seek to formulate this principle. An open communion is legitimate if:

a. **There is a private personal interest in receiving
the sacrament, not a general one for always and
everywhere.**[1] Obviously, not every instance where there
is expressed interest in receiving the sacrament can legitimize open communion (as is always the case in such an
encounter); otherwise it would be pointless that certain
conditions would be required for those cases that are specifically permitted. On the other hand, however, the risk of
death[e] cannot be considered to be the only situation
of special interest. It is unclear why only such a risk of
death could justify such a special interest. Certainly,
in the common sensibility, as in the Code of Canon Law,
the danger of death demands a special interest in the question of receiving the sacraments, but that interest cannot
be demonstrated to be absolutely unique unless one wishes
to hold the opinion that there are cases in which salvation is
absolutely guaranteed by a sacramental act. The fact that
the closeness of death puts a person in a situation in which

---

1. These bolded forms are my addition to make clear that these complete his
thought as theses that are then explained.

they, although they still live, are somewhat "exempt" in terms of ecclesiastical sign-value, seems to me to be making an ad hoc assumption. On the other hand, one could just as easily say that it is precisely a dying person who must most strongly realize their membership of the church as a sign of their salvation. In addition, the church's own legislation obviously considers cases to be possible that have nothing to do with a dying person in principle.

b. **If the defect in the ecclesiastical character is negative and not positive (privative).** This distinction seems understandable to me and fundamental to our question. I call a lack of ecclesiastical sign-character for the unity of confession and faith positive (privative) when, in the specific circumstances in which the reception of the sacrament takes place, this sacrament is understood as making confessional differences unimportant and an indifference or equivalency is postulated between the various churches—that is, the differences regarding belief that actually exist between the participants in open communion and the denominational separateness that also exists between them. Where, from the concrete circumstances, an objective or, to some extent, even a subjective demonstration is given that these differences in themselves or at least with regard to receiving the sacrament are considered an indifferent matter, an open communion is certainly illegitimate; otherwise, an intercommunion without any border would be legitimate. On the other hand, there are cases (under the assumptions of point a above) in which such a demonstration is not given in the concrete circumstances, and the lack of full ecclesial sign-character is thus negative and privative. Such a merely negative defect is undoubtedly possible in principle. For there are certainly cases of receiving the sacraments in which neither the administrator nor the recipient suspect themselves to consider the differences in faith and church affiliation to be an indifferent matter between themselves regarding sacramental sharing. If such cases did not exist, then any open communion would be impossible, for no private interest in receiving the sacrament can legitimize such a positive explanation of a dogmatic and ecclesiological indifferentism. Of course, in the concrete case, the boundaries between the positive (privative) and the merely negative lack of ecclesial sign-character in receiving the Sacrament are not very easy to draw. But this results simply from the nature of a sign whose constitution, and not just the subsequent interpretation, includes the understanding of the ecclesial community itself. However, this understanding is variable depending on the general social situation and also the private situation of those directly involved. The same physical events in a particular situation, depending on the circumstances, may be a demonstration of the indifferentism described above; they may not be in other situations. Nor ought it be denied that positive legal assertions on the part of the church also contribute to this variable meaning of the sign, even if these do not alone determine the concrete meaning of such a sign in a particular situation. (Perhaps the understanding of what is meant can be aided by the analogous case of ancestor veneration in China and Japan. The same ritual process could once have the character of a religious rite in one concrete environment and, without changing materially, could transform itself into a civil rite by changing the mental and social situation. And precisely this transformation could be codetermined by the fact that the church declared the rite to be a mere bourgeois ceremony, thereby giving it this very character.)

4. Whether there is a merely negative lack of ecclesial symbolism in a case of intercommunion or a positive (privative)

one depends not only, but also, on the extent to which the non-Catholic sacramental recipient and the actual Catholic participants in such a communion possess the actual ability or inability to understand the confessional faith-differences regarding the nature of the sacraments and the church. Of course, in such an open communion, the Catholic minister is always actively involved, of whom a positive explicit knowledge of the significance of the differences in faith and belief about the church can of course be expected. But here, too, the feeling of an indifferentist interpretation of what one is doing in open communion is at least possible. For the other participants in such an open communion, however, the possibility that this might be understood as a demonstration of dogmatic or ecclesiastical indifferentism depends on whether they really know and understand such differences in their concrete consciousness of faith and church, and if they then consider these to be an indifferent matter both theologically and regarding salvation. However, one must now admit quite soberly that such confessional differences are hardly ever realized by the large number who may be involved in an intercommunion. It is for this reason that people argue for permission for communion to be given. Of course, an intercommunion under these circumstances may then give rise to a certain danger that this crowd, to which such differences are more or less unknown or only indirectly known through the experience of church division and the differences it makes visible, would regard these communities as being, in principle, equivalent. In particular cases, such a danger must certainly be seen and taken into account using discretionary judgment about where the boundaries lie between a private and merely negative lack of ecclesial sign-character. But also, in this deficiency, which in fact exists among the current mass of believers who no longer simply receive their faith from the society which forms them, there is a presumption that in their situation, there is no demonstrated dogmatic and ecclesiastical indifferentism but a positive lack of the ecclesial sign-character exists. Of course, this does not apply to cases, as is clear from what has just been said, in which ministers from both confessional sides would hold a common eucharistic celebration. (On this topic, more will be said in point 2 in the next section below, with certain reservations.) The theological question, which is not merely social or having to do with the psychology of religion but also truly theological—that is, how such a lack of a dogmatic awareness of denominational differences can be the case in the multitude of believers of all confessions—cannot be further addressed here. Except to speculate that this lack has a great significance, beyond what has already been said for our question, also for the whole problem of ecumenism. In my opinion, it could be conclusively shown that in this regard, one does not rely on the appeal to a *fides implicita*, because in many cases at least that religious relation to a strictly dogmatic commitment of one's own church is lacking, and one's own church affiliation, even if one is quite content with it, is more or less clearly interpreted as a historical coincidence of birth or upbringing.

5. Intercommunion, therefore, seems to be fundamentally forbidden only where it implies, in the public sphere, an undeniable commitment to the fundamental equivalency of different confessions regarding the sacraments and the church. If we say "only," then it does not imply that such a case of an illegitimate intercommunion is only a marginal case. Because and insofar as a fully developed understanding of faith must be demanded from the people in question, because the sacraments have an ecclesial aspect of attesting to unity in faith and in the church, the rejection of intercommunion and therefore of open communion must be the initial position. An open communion must then be legitimized according to the principles that we tried to develop under

point 3 above. In this regard, it should again be pointed out that for such a legitimacy of intercommunion, the consent of the church is in principle necessary, because only such a statement makes it sufficiently clear that this situation is only a case of the negative lack of the ecclesiastical sign-character of sacramental reception. Here the question can be left open as to who can receive such ecclesial permission in various cases. The less such an open communion is noticeable in the public sphere of the church, and the less the danger of an indifferentist interpretation becomes, the more likely it is that this permission and the one receiving it can probably be considered as falling into the purview of the church's ministers.

Norms to Guide Current Practice

1. According to the basic norms suggested, it is self-evident that unbaptized persons cannot be admitted to the Eucharist.
2. It goes without saying that intercommunion cannot be allowed with the equal participation of the ministers of several confessions. For, at least in most cases, this would be a demonstration that there is no real schism among the churches. Such a schism must be evaluated theologically. Whether it is possible that there be individual cases in which such a demonstration would not be made in concrete circumstances, and therefore the matter could be decided differently, can be left as an open question. But the presence of such an event, which is conceivable, would have to be confirmed by an explicit or tacit agreement from the ecclesiastical authorities, it seems to me. But such an ordinary intercommunion would normally just be a demonstration of the theological and religious insignificance of the differences between the separate churches' understandings of the sacraments and ecclesiology. If these churches were reduced to being understood as insignificant different external organizations of Christianity, this would

elevate the actual understanding of the faith of each of the members of the individual churches to an absolute principle of an exclusive nature; it would only obscure the very radical differences that exist in Christian faith-consciousnesses (regarding the sacraments and ecclesiology in particular), which sooner or later would nevertheless reemerge and produce worse church divisions than those we are complaining about now. Wherever subjective belief, without being tied back to that of a larger community of faith, is absolutized and becomes the only norm, while it may counterfeit unity for a while, in the long run will prove divisive. In the case of an absolute intercommunion, separate communities of sympathy would soon form at the grassroots, which would be even less interconnected than the now separated churches. Of course, this basic principle does not adequately answer the question of what the church officials should do if de facto such intercommunion occurs with the participation of public officials of several churches. This question is difficult to answer because ministry in the church must strive to not only be fundamentally correct but also effective declarations, but by a simple condemnation of such intercommunions, they are not already eo ipso eliminated from the world.

3. When considering an intercommunion that has a more private character, and that has only a negative lack of ecclesial character in regard to the same understanding of the sacrament and the concept of the church, a certain amount of generosity and tolerance seems to have a place. Here one should give the well-considered discretion of the individual pastor a certain leeway. While he would have to ensure that such open communion (at marriages and other ceremonies) does not become simply the admission of an unlimited crowd or merely a bourgeois convention, one should not be anxious in such cases, nor should one require explicit permission to be granted in all cases from the bishop or from Rome. Such

a strict rule actually remains ineffective, does not seem to be absolutely necessary, and would only create unrest in people's consciences without preventing cases of this sort from occurring. Of course, even in such cases, a certain consensus of a religious and theological nature is required of those involved in the sacramental events, but one should not require more here than can be seriously expected given the constitution of the participants. If the non-Catholic Christian seriously and decisively wants to participate in the Lord's Supper, then in such a case, this seems sufficient. One can leave the rest to the faith implicit in such a desire, a *fides implicita*, and not require him to articulate this belief that he cannot understand and that even most Catholic Christians do not know.

4. Where there are cases in which the line between a merely negative and a positively privative lack of unity is no longer clear, a positive and explicit permission on the part of church officials would be required, of course, so that the ambiguities regarding the character of this intercommunion can be clarified. Of course, such a permission (given the existing necessary conditions) may also take on the character of demonstrating the relevance of dogmatic differences among those who take part. Where such permission is deemed necessary, given, and accepted, the danger of misunderstanding the resulting intercommunion is certainly largely eliminated.

5. The cases of open communion expressly permitted by Rome would then have to be considered to determine which analogous, but not expressly stated, other cases they have or may have alongside them that have a right to equal treatment. It would then have to be further examined whether such cases are already permitted by the Roman decrees in an *analogia iuris* or whether they still require a separate permit from Rome or from the competent bishop (a possibility that is also foreseen within the Roman decrees).

Notes

from the Sämtliche Werke edition

Chapter 1: Asking the Question, Imagining an Answer

a. *Reform und Anerkennung kirchlicher Ämter*, Ein Memorandum der Arbeitsgemein-schaft Ökumenischer Universitätsinstitute (Munich: Mainz, 1973). Cf. in this volume [i.e., Karl Rahner, "Vom Sinn und Auftrag des kirchlichen Amtes," in *Sämtliche Werke*, vol. 27, *Einheit in Vielfalt*, ed. Karl Lehmann and Albert Raffelt (Freiburg: Herder, 2002)—Trans.], pp. 146–49.

b. "Stellungsnahme der Glaubenskommission der Bischöfe," *Herder Korrespondenz* 27 (1973): 159.

c. Cf. Hans Küng, "Im Interesse der Sache. Antwort an Karl Rahner," in *Fehlbar?*, ed. Küng (Zürich: Benzinger, 1973), 19–68; esp. 52–54.

Chapter 2: The Essence of the Church's Structure

a. This story is about Edmund Schlink (1903–84). Cf. Karl Rahner's comment in Paul M. Zulehner, "Denn du kommst unserem Tun mit deiner Gnade zuvor . . . ," in *Zur Theologie der Seelsorge heute. Paul M. Zulehner im Gespräch mit Karl Rahner*, by Zulehner with Rahner (Düsseldorf, 1984), 88: "Edmund Schlink hat mir einmal gesagt: Sie machen mir doch nicht weis, daß, wenn drei Christen in Sibirien Eucharistie feiern und es nach euren Regeln kein Pfarrer dabei, dies keine wahre Eucharistie wäre."

b. Heinrich Denzinger, *Enchiridion symbolorum definitionum et declarationum de rebus fidei et morum* (hereafter cited as DH), 43rd ed., ed. Peter Hunermann (Freiburg: Herder, 2001) 1648.

c. Heinz Robert Schlette, *Kommunikation und Sakrament: Theologische Deutung der geistlichen Kommunion*, Quaestiones Disputatae 8 (Freiburg: Herder, 1960).

d. Cf. DH 4530–41. Cf. Congregation for the Doctrine of the Faith, "Mysterium ecclesiae," Declaration, June 24, 1973.

e. Which particular session of the council Rahner means cannot be discerned, for discussion of the problem of the relationship of primacy and episcopacy occupied the council from the beginning. It already appears, for example, in the critique of ecclesiological Schema I produced by Semmelroth and Rahner. The discussion certainly reached a high point in the fall of 1963 with the discussion of the passages of Schema II on the church related to this topic (§§16–21). At this point, Rahner was a member of the ecclesiological subcommission Va (*De collegio et ministeriis Episcoporum*), which was dedicated to this question in particular; it produced the relevant texts in service to its mission. They are collected by Günther Wassilowsky: *Universales Heilssakrament Kirche: Karl Rahners Beitrag zur Ekklesiology des II. Vatikanums*, Innsbrucker theologisches Studien 59 (Innsbruck, 2001), 236–45. See particularly 243f. We thank Dr. Wassilowsky for bringing this text to attention.

f. Cyprian of Carthage, *Epistula* 71, in *Corpus Scriptorum Ecclesiasticorum Latinorum* (hereafter cited as CSEL), 3.2, pp. 771–74; in German, *Bibliothek der Kirchenväter* (hereafter cited as BKV), 1.60, pp. 327–31. Cf. K. Rahner, *Die Bußlehre Cyprians von Karthago*, in *Schriften zur Theologie*, vol. 11 (Zürich: Benzinger Verlag, 1973), 224–324, esp. 228ff.

g. Hans Habe (1911–77), journalist and writer.

h. Arthur Vermeersch and Joseph Creusen, *Epitome Iuris Canonici cum commentariis ad scholas et ad usum privatum*, 3 vols. (Rome: Mechliniae, 1936), 3:10: "Si vero a fide, tamquam privatus, deficeret, quod plerique reputant impossibile, ipso facto sua suprema potestate destitueretur, quippe qui voluntarie e sinu Ecclesiae exiret."

i. Code of Canon Law (hereafter cited as CIC) 1917, can. 1556: "Prima Sedes a nemine iudicatur."

j. See. K. Rahner, "Reflection on the Concept of *ius divinum* in Catholic Thought," in *Theological Investigations*, vol. 5 (Baltimore: Darton, Longman & Todd, 1966), 219–43, originally published "Über den Begriff des *jus divinum* im katholischen Verständnis," in *Schriften zur Theologie*, vol. 5 (Einsiedeln: Benzinger Verlag, 1962), 249–77.

k. See Augustine, *Contra Iulianum* 5.11.45; Thomas Aquinas, *ST* III, q. 61, a. 3. See also Leo Scheffczyk, "Natursakrament," in *Lexikon für Theologie und Kirche* (hereafter cited as LThK), 3rd ed. (Freiburg: Herder, 1993), 7:696f.

Chapter 3: Recognizing Reality

a. CIC 1917 can. 1098:

> Si haberi vel adiri nequeat sine gravi incommodo parochus vel Ordinarius vel sacerdos delegatus qui matrimonio assistant ad normam cononum 1095, 1096; 1° In mortis periculo validum et licitum est matrimonium contractum coram solis testibus; et etiam extra mortis

periculum, dummodo prudenter praevideatur eam rerum conditionem esse per mensem duraturam; 2° In utroque casu, si praesto sit alius sacerdos qui adesse possit, vocari et, una cum testibus, matrimonio assistere debet, salva coniugii validate coram solis testibus.

If the pastor or Ordinary or delegated priest who assists at marriage according to the norm of Canons 1095 and 1096 cannot be had or cannot be present without grave inconvenience: 1° In danger of death marriage is contracted validly and licitly in the presence only of witnesses; and outside of danger of death provided it is prudently foreseen that this condition will perdure for one month; 2° In either case, if another priest can be present, he shall be called and together with the witnesses must assist at marriage, with due regard for conjugal validity solely in the presence of witnesses.

Translation from Peters, *1917 Pio-Benedictine Code*. Cf. can. 1116 in the 1983 code, which is substantially the same.

Chapter 4: Sharing Salvation

a. DH 4530.

b. Cf. LThK.E. 1:352f. See also DH 4354.

c. LThK.E. 1:352f.: "Evidens est quod haec 'communio' *in vita* Ecclesiae, secundum adiuncta temporum, applicata est, priusquam *in iure* velut codificat fuerit"—"It is evident that this 'communion' was applied in the church's *life* according to the circumstances of the time, before it was codified *as law*." Also DH 4354.

d. Joseph Ratzinger, "Kommentar zu den 'Bekanntmachungen, die der Generalsekretär des Konzils in der 123. Generalkongregation am 16. November 1964 mitgeteilt hat,'" in LThK.E. 1: 348–59; here 353.

e. In the original, wrongly printed as "rechtschaffen" = justifying (verb) instead of "rechtschaffend" = justifying (adj.).

f. *Lumen gentium*, in LThK.E. 1:172f.; DH 4119.

g. Cyprian of Carthage, *Epistula* 71.2, in CSEL 3.2, pp. 722f.; in German, BKV 1.60, p. 329.

h. Cf. Ernst Dassmann, "Character," in *Augustinus-Lexikon*, vol. 1 (Basel, 1980–94), 835–40.

i. DH 4541.

j. Cf. Karl Rahner, "Laienbeichte," in LThK² 6:741–42.

Chapter 5: Form, Validity, and History

a. Cf. The *Ordo initionis christianae adultorum* (Vatican, 1973); in German, *Die Feier der Eingliderung Erwachsener in die Kirche nach dem neuen Rituale Romanum* (Freiburg-Einsiedeln, 1975); in English, *Rite of Christian Initiation of Adults.*

Chapter 6: Bearing Our Divisions on the Way to Unity

a. DH 4139; LThK.E. 1, pp. 202ff.

Appendix: An Excursus on Intercommunion

a. Cf. K. Rahner, "Reflection on the Concept of *ius divinum* in Catholic Thought," in *Theological Investigations*, vol. 5, trans. Karl Heins Kruger (New York: Crossroad, 1970), 219–43.
b. Original "keinen Zweifel" changed by German editors to "kein Zweifel."
c. Original "offenbar dann" changed in German edition to prevent a repetition of the word *dann.*
d. Original "welche" changed to "welcher" by German editor.
e. Cf. CIC 1917 can. 854 §2; can. 864–66.

Other Related Works by Karl Rahner

This list includes works by Rahner that refer to *Vorfragen zu einem ökumenischen Amtsverständnis* and several works of related topic.

Sämtliche Werke, vol. 27, *Einheit in Vielfalt*, ed. Karl Lehmann and Albert Raffelt (Freiburg: Herder, 2002).
   "Vom Sinn und Auftrag des kirchlichen Amtes," 146–149. Originally published *Frankfurter Allgemeine Zeitung*, no. 38 (February 14 1973): 9.
Theological Investigations, vol. 5, trans. Karl Heinz Kruger (London: Helicon Press, 1966).
   "Reflection on the Concept of *ius divinum* in Catholic Thought," 219–243.
Theological Investigations, vol. 14, trans. David Bourke (London: Darton, Longman & Todd, 1976).
   "On the Theology of a Pastoral Synod," 116–134.
   "Aspects of the Episcopal Office," 185–201.
   "How the Priest Should View His Official Ministry," 202–219.
Theological Investigations, vol. 17, trans. Margaret Kohl (New York: Crossroad, 1981).
   "Mysterium ecclesiae," 139–155 [slightly edited]. Originally published *Stimmen der Zeit* 191 (1973): 579–594.
   "Transformations in the Church and Secular Society," 167–180.
   "Third Church? Christians between the Churches," 215–227.

Theological Investigations, vol. 18, trans. Edward Quinn (New York: Crossroad, 1983).

> "Pseudo-problems in Ecumenical Discussion" (lecture at the Seventh Ecumenical Congress of Jesuits in Frankfurt am Main, August 27, 1977), 35–53.

Theological Investigations, vol. 22, trans. Joseph Donceel (London: Herder & Herder, 1991).

> "Understanding the Priestly Office," 208–213.
>
> > *Note*: This article begins with Rahner thinking back to the *Vorfragen* and noting that it did not receive much attention. The article, originally written for a Festschrift for Heinrich Fries, constitutes "an outline of the considerations that belong to this group of questions."

Lightning Source UK Ltd.
Milton Keynes UK
UKHW040645120822
407211UK00001B/140

9 781506 484297